IF THE
CAP FITS

AND BEYOND

K.H.BROWN

Editing, design, typesetting and publishing by UK Book Publishing.
www.ukbookpublishing.com
ISBN: 978-1-917329-74-3

PREFACE

Keith Brown entered this world under the following circumstances. It is believed Fay Rothwell who worked in an armaments factory in Upminster, Essex, during the war was the main negotiator in Keith's adoption. Fay's first husband had been killed when his ship, HMS Hunter, was sunk in a Norwegian Fiord during the Second World War. Fay had a sister who it is believed was unable to have children; her name was Rose. During Fay's working day her sister looked after her daughter, Sandra. Rose adored Sandra and they formed a bond. Unfortunately, the babysitting arrangement came to an end when Fay returned home one day after work and heard her daughter calling Rose, MUM. Fay knew a young 18-year-old girl who was pregnant to an Englishman unnamed on Keith's birth certificate. The girl, whose name was Hilda Finne, was originally from Sweden we think. She helped to set up the adoption through Fay to have Keith adopted by Rose and her husband Howard. But Keith was not the cute Sandra, which led to some harsh discipline.

Seventy-eight years later Keith remembers his early years following his adoption.

His adopted mother had been an East-end barmaid. Nastier than the Krays. Victorian in her discipline. Keith recalls being taken to hospital after Mum had punched him. He fell backwards onto an open cupboard door; these doors were very thin and made of metal as were most cupboards in a prefab initially built as an overflow estate on Harold Hill in Essex. He was taken to hospital and as they were travelling there, all his mum could say, and repeat, was that he had fallen, and it was an accident. At that age he didn't know why she was so insistent. Pity he kept his mouth shut as things might have turned out much better Some things are set in his mind when at the age of seven or eight he was given a tiny suitcase, put outside the front gate of their prefab in Harold Hill and told to go and find his real mother. The second time this happened, Keith walked off to his best friend's house. Albert Plummer and his family all knew what Keith's mother was like, and Mrs Plummer was always so kind to him. Staying the night, Keith in later years could only surmise Mrs Plummer had made some kind of contact with Rose as no police had been alerted, to his knowledge. Rose never did that again. Secretly Keith longed to be the son of Mrs Plummer. This increased as he visited Albert several times a week – their prefab was about 250 yards away on a different part of the estate from Keith's prefab. Mrs Plummer had two slightly protruded front teeth. By some quirk of fate in later years Keith dated Mrs Plummer's niece completely by accident but it was not to last. She also had the slight protrusion of teeth and he refrained from calling her "Bugs" as he was not yet mature enough.

The beatings for minor child antics declined as Keith won the Romford and District Boxing championship in 1960 (at six stone two ounces). He never retaliated during her windmill arm waving attacks; he just grabbed her wrists.

IF THE CAP FITS
AND BEYOND

The Beginning

Aged 15, I started work on British Railways and was based in the Linesman's Hut at Ilford Station in Essex. One of my relatives was the Station Master at King's Cross Railway Station so some strings were pulled, and this was the beginning of me being in grown up land. Initially I was sent to West Ham Tech one day a week to begin an ONC in Electronic Engineering. Never happened! Much of the time the teacher never turned up, so it was no surprise that my prowess in card playing improved.

The only significant occurrence during what they called my probationship, during my early days in the grown-up world, was when I got angry with one of the grownups and decided to make a bomb. Not the usual kind, just a schoolboy gadget. Condensed milk tin with small stones to hold the thing down. A bag of flour taped to the tin and finally one BIG firework. (The ones with a red coned end to put it into the ground.) This cone was inserted in the flour bag. I showed the marvellous device to one of the men who tolerated me, and he promptly said take it outside and take it apart. Blast!! And it did! Just needed to see what would happen. My initial thought was that the firework would go off and the bad man would be covered in flour. Oh dear! I lit it and stood back. A huge bang erupted; the firework took off, landing in the four feet (between the rails). There were of course explosive devices used on the railways to tell trains to stop due to men working on the lines. These devices were clipped to the rails possibly a quarter of a mile from the workers and went off as the train wheels went over them. The signalman in his box just 70 yards away from my launch pad thought that the explosion was one of those devices and promptly put all the signals to Red. So, I inadvertently stopped the Hook Continental on the Main Down Line and the electric lines, just before Ilford Station, and everyone was very angry. Except me!

More drama and trauma! Two small incidents involving near death. When I was awaiting some communication from my fellow workers, I went into childhood mode. Just outside Manor Park railway station there was a cemetery with a high spiked wrought iron fence (railing) separating the railway from the place of no return. I noted the wonderous array of conker trees festooned with conkers. I sat on a very large electric cable supported by cable bearers just a foot away from the fence. Right, I thought, step onto the horizontal part of the fence, jump over and get harvesting. Unfortunately, having put one foot on the railing I hadn't given the necessary push to allow me to jump onto the railing and enter conker heaven. I fell backwards onto the cable which catapulted me forwards. In a split second the spikes were about to enter my stomach. Instinctively I tried to grab between the spikes on the horizontal bar. Having missed by a mile suddenly both hands were impaled. As one worker said later, it looked like I had crucified myself, I noted I was losing quite a bit of blood. In panic and with gritted teeth, I raised both arms and released myself from the railings. Luckily neither spike had completely penetrated either hand but there were two large brake dust filled holes. (Brake dust from the train brakes being applied before entering the railway station.)

A fellow worker grabbed me by the shoulders and started to walk me towards a shunter's hut dangerously situated across four main lines to and from London. "Don't faint on me," he said. An ambulance was called and yes, the arrival time was as bad as it is now. Three quarters of an hour before the ambulance arrived, at which time shock had encouraged me to lie down for a bit. The bleeding had stopped. Luck prevailed as at the hospital and after some rather painful cleaning of the wounds it was noted that luckily the spike that had entered my right hand in the fleshy part between my thumb and index finger and only required a couple of stitches. The left hand was less fortunate as although no bones were severed, the spike had entered between my pinkie and wedding ring finger. My little finger for several months resembled a Mr Spock minor salute. All hell was let loose when I was not accompanied by anyone to the hospital or indeed back. I walked back from the hospital, left arm in a sling. The four stitches deemed I was going to have real trouble riding my Lambretta LI 150 form Harold Wood Station back home. The clutch was very, very stiff, and of course on the left of the handlebars. What made it worse was the grip. Once the lever had been squeezed (the clutch) it had to be rotated into each gear. Can anyone see the problem? Well done! I had the left arm in a sling. I made it home by using both hands to squeeze the clutch lever and to change gear. It hurt! After a quick explanation at home, I just couldn't resist going out and bragging to anyone I knew what had happened. I was getting pretty good at riding the scooter and everyone wanted to see the stitches, but I could only expose the right-hand bandage enough for them to see the results of my heroic not-conker encounter.

Gorgeous summer's day about 150 yards from Forest Gate Signal Box. Once again leaning against a big cable but not sitting on it. (Can anyone see the lack of supervision by my work colleagues?) My feet were touching a railway sleeper and I had a bit of a shut eye coming on. The Hook Continental steam train (Britannia Class, I think) came hurtling down the track less than 100 yards away and luck was with me as the train driver saw me and hooted. I had no time to stand up so the only chance I would have would be if I pulled my legs back but not raise them. I hoped that the running boards on the carriages were uniform as the first one cleared my knees by about three inches. It seemed like an eternity as I crouched there terrified. I think by this time at Ilford's Lineman Hut everyone including the Chief Lineman whose name I believe was "Jim Symes", decided I was better suited with another department. So, I was sent to Stratford and joined the Cable Jointers unit. There I did learn a lot including how to play Solo. Two and a half years had passed without too much trauma, but it seems I had some talent in cable jointing, and I was complimented during the DC/AC rewiring of the signal relays controlling the Signals and railway points during the DC to AC changeover around 1960. However, I felt I was getting nowhere and life at home had not improved especially as Mum was taking £2.00 of my £4.60 a week for – as she would say – "paying for my keep". A lesson in how to manage my money.

This poor attempt at a sort of book started when Mother said, "Why don't you join the Army like your uncle Art/Hart?" Who knows his name, as my mother's East-end accent gave no clue? "I have," I answered. "What?" she screamed as my dad came in from his work situated in Canning Town at the Paragon Works as a printer's reader. "What has the silly bugger done now?" he said. Looking at him I said, "I've joined the Army."

It all started when Barbara was hanging about with the usual crowd in our large, new, overflow estate shopping centre. I think we called it Hildene shops. I don't recall his name but there stood a fine-looking soldier with Royal Signals in a curved shape white lettering on a Royal Blue background, just at the top of his shoulders. His gleaming belt buckle attaching the Blanco belt and highly polished boots, and finally the beret with Certa Cito hat badge, a depiction of Mercury standing on the world. (Certa Cito) Swift and Sure. He was wearing Battle Dress. He explained he was on leave having done basic training and was going back to do his trade training in Catterick the following week. I looked at Barbara who was obviously smitten by the uniform. As she strutted her stuff down to Woolworths, my mind was made up. If the uniform could attract someone like Barbara, then that's for me. The next words from this strapping soldier were, "Yer, I got a SMG, and I fired an SLR". Not a man of even modest amount of language skills.

That would be fun, I thought. Roy Bishop, my best mate, and I boarded the bus and set off for Romford where the Recruitment Office resided. We were ushered into a room to do some tests. At that time, I thought I could get 100% as the test could be passed by a 10-year-old. Maths and English I recall. We both passed and were told to report back on the 13 October 1962 for a medical. Currently Mum and Dad were unaware of what was about to be a change in their lives. Roy and I entered the Recruitment Centre on the 13th. There was the smiling recruitment Sergeant we had met before. He smiled and ushered us in to see the doc. Having had the tapping of back and chest, the stethoscope trying to find my heart, open mouth, Ah! Eyes peered at and ears investigated, I was horrified when asked to take our trousers down and our pants. Cold hands cupped each ball as I was asked to cough. Glad that was over we were ushered back into the office and told by our kindly Sergeant that once we had accepted the Queen's shilling and swore the oath we were now in the Army. Our results on the tests were good and we could join whatever branch of the army we wanted to. **Roy wanted to join the Tank Regiment. WHAT?** Roy, I know we are not in yet but what are you going to do when you have done your time? Where do you get a job driving bloody tanks when you are back in civvy street? Great! Roy saw the light! Now, said the Sergeant, we must see the captain (OC) who was in command of the centre. Lovely! A knock on the OC's door which was met with a shout, "Come in". The Sergeant's demeanour changed. Shouting Left, right left, Halt! Quite a shock as we were now facing a GOD. After a short explanation of our forthcoming training, GOD directed us to the paperwork, and we signed whatever was placed in front of us and swore the oath to the Queen and country. "Stand up straight," shouted GOD from behind his desk. "You're in the Army now!" I do believe we were given at that time a Queen's Shilling, so no going back now.

In the main office we were given our leave passes as we were to report to Catterick on the 30th October 1962. Along with a rail warrant. We both headed home. Roy and I headed for the shops and to my delight the gang were there and Barbara. Guess what? We have joined the army. We showed our paperwork but unfortunately Barbara did not react as before. Maybe I was too short.

Mum played her trump card. She noted that she or Dad had to sign the paperwork as I was not yet 18, the age at which you could make your own mind up. I was only three months from being 18. Dad in an unlikely action for a subservient husband took the permission form and promptly signed it. For months Mum tried to get me to buy myself out of the army for £20.00 which you could do I believe within a certain time following initial enlistment. I did not.

Roy and I put our suitcases on the rack in the carriage. The huge steam train, the type that had a famous person's name in the centre of the main boiler above the wheel arch if I recall, awaited permission to depart. The engine "bellowed" steam (if that is the right word), over the platform before we headed out "Up North". We headed out to Darlington from King's Cross. Our only sense of humour moment was when a very good-looking woman also appeared in the carriage. The young woman had shapely long legs and quite a short skirt. Drawn to the legs and a bit of elbow nudging, Roy and I struggled to keep ourselves from sniggering. This Aphrodite vision was wearing an ankle bracelet. Where we were brought up and being sixties MEN (lol), we were told that only prostitutes wore ankle bracelets. As soon as the woman noticed our nudging a slight smile appeared on her face. I often wondered what she was thinking. Also, was it true about the ankle bracelet thing? We arrived in Darlington knowing we had to get a train to Richmond. Sadly, the old Richmond station is now a garden centre-cum-coffee area with a swimming pool. The railway track ripped up, but now, a haven for dog walkers doing a circular walk through Easby Abbey having crossed the old railway bridge and the River Swale. Having made the connection, we arrived in Richmond. I was astonished, what a beautiful town, and still is to this day with its castle and cobbled streets. The town square at that time housed the Green Howards Museum. Finally, the waterfall and the view down what I was told was the fastest running river in Britain.

Several of us stood by the station entrance, cases ready to be loaded onto our transport to Catterick Garrison. Of course, there was nobody there to pick us up. A sign with a number to call for new arrivals. We called but got no answer. Just moments later a 3-Tonner (Bedford army truck) arrived dropping off something at the station, possibly Royal Mail. The soldier unloading the mail offered to take us to our new homes. Now it starts!!!

Arriving at 11 Signal Regiment we entered the middle Sandhurst Block which was to be our home for the next six weeks. The 20-man room with our one wardrobe, iron bed and bedding were to be our luxury furnished accommodation.

Day One. 6.00 am. My slumber was rudely awakened by the banging of dustbin lids and the screeching of the drill staff. We all had to line up in the corridor and answer our names which were called out by the Lance Corporals. Apparently, you had to come to attention before answering

"Yes, Corporal". Having washed we headed to the cookhouse. I wondered what the day would bring but was strangely excited.

At that time Cilla Black's record "Anyone who had a heart" was playing in the junior rank's clubs. I was a Sandie Shaw fan. "Puppet on a string". How apt I thought!

I could not believe the kit we had to carry back to our rooms from the Quartermaster's where we were kitted out. In addition to measuring for our Dress uniform, Battledress kit was issued including suitcase, kitbag, webbing including small and large backpacks, sea kitbag, boots, shoes, hat/beret shirts, PT dress, tie, underpants including long johns…anyway I won't go on. New language for me as the staff put the items on the counter "Boots, size eight for the use of." Each time the same comment, "for the use of" after each issue of clothing. I dropped my small backpack unknown to me and when we all got back, we were all told to check we had not lost something. I raced to the troop office and banged on the door shouting it was my backpack. Well, this lieutenant came thundering out and shouted at me and frankly terrified me!! Having vented on me, Sgt Sixsmith, our Troop Sergeant, came out with my pack and became a fatherlike figure as he smiled at me and handed the backpack and said," run along and be more careful in future". I will never forget his kindness and reassurance until I die.

The first day was much like many others for the first six weeks other than we were assigned our army numbers; mine was easier than most – 23927973, nice duplications of four numbers. I was fit in those days, so the road runs and gym work came easily to me. In fact, the education classes also were interesting learning about NATO and other military organisations. Drill was ok until we had the beginnings of one of the coldest winters recorded (so I believe). During drill periods we were not allowed to wear gloves. We held our self-loading rifles in various positions on the march or at a standstill. Some men were crying with the cold. During one of these drills one of the trainees marched off the square. The drill Sergeant stood stunned but within a few seconds marched us all off the square. I don't think I ever saw that recruit again. My other cold memory of that harsh winter was when a poor sad-looking lad who was attempting to traverse a rope between two telegraph poles over a four-foot ditch and of course full of water concealed by ice, lost his grip on the rope and fell through the ice and was waist deep in freezing water. We were only allowed a PT vest, shorts, and PT pumps in those days. PT staff raged at him and sent him across again after dragging him out. He shivered and made it about two feet across until he lost his grip yet again. Finally, the poor waif was dragged off and we never saw him again.

Big day when we were allowed outside of barracks having been given our cap badges. The Royal Signals cap badge comes in two parts: Mercury and the Crown. Now as a real soldier having avoided shooting anything other than a target, I prepared for trade training at 8th Signal Regiment after a spot of leave. "Pass off" was a big deal and rows of folding chairs were lined up on the square for the proud relatives of 9 and 10 troop Signallers that had successfully got through basic training. I looked but couldn't see my parents and of course why was I not surprised when I realised – they were not there.

Not much to relate as I knocked on the door at 63 Cricklade Avenue, Harold Hill, Essex. Dad answered the door and Rose from hell continued to offer to buy me out of the Army. Rather glad I was travelling back to Catterick after a few weeks at home. My British railways cable jointing skills were about to pay dividends.

Initial Trade Training for Cable jointers was conducted in wooden spiders (not the insect type) on Whinny Hill. Mr Calendar, whose deputy I was to become many years later, gave the introductory welcome. I can't recall the number of weeks we were to be in trade training but recall being his coffin bearer and always remember silly little things about him such as the fact he was also a football referee and laid claim to fame for having sent off Jackie Charlton for a foul committed during a Football League game. He also gave me some of his old notes when I started as an instructor and when I attended Middlesbrough Polytechnic College, completing my ONC in Electrical and Electronic Engineering. He was well liked by everyone (possible exception... Jackie Charlton).

Unwelcome news: there was no Cable Jointers Course running. I went to see Mr Calendar and said I would buy myself out as I had only joined up to be a Cable Jointer. Lineman at that time only dealt with overhead cable (pole work etc) and some equipments plus the good old D10 telephone and 10 pair cable installations. Norman (Mr C) said if I could get four other volunteers to change trade, he would run the course. I raced around promoting Cable Jointing as a far superior trade especially for when discharge or retirement eventually arrived. Game on! We were about to meet Mr Mac.

Mr MacSkimming was the Cable jointing civilian instructor. Might have misspelled his name, could have been McSkimming. Doesn't matter because we all called him Mac. Over the years that followed whenever we met at the Trade Training School, he always greeted me by saying "How you are doing, Brownie?". Having been given a jointing task I always finished miles ahead of the class, so we were used to chatting. Me and my lowly aspirations, and his moaning about a lot of things. At the end of the trade training course, we were told whoever came top in the written exam would be given the chance to continue onto the B2 course which was about to start. (Quick note. The B trades went from B3 to B1.) Similar for Education (Army Certificate of Education) ACE 3 to ACE 1 (more about his much later). These qualifications also were needed for promotion.

Last day of the B3 Cable Jointers course the results were in. There was a Scots guy who was not especially good at Jointing but that didn't matter – it was the written exam results that would gift the B2 chance (more trade money). Everyone gathered around for the results of the written exam. When his name came out, he had somehow managed to get 96% (did not count on other people studying) but then Signalman Brown, 97%. Wow! I was on the B2 course, and the rest of the guys posted to wherever. I admit Mr Mac and I just continued as usual during the practical B2 training, and I just eased off when it came to the written stuff.

Last weekend in Richmond with a Sergeant who had no sense in coming along with us. After a stomach full of beer, various vomiting incidents, I found myself in a tattoo shop. Left wrist. A small butterfly, stung like crazy. The cost: my last two shillings and sixpence which meant a walk back to barracks. Luckily the Sergeant paid for a taxi for us drunks. Well so that is what a Sergeant is for! Sadly, all the bright colours have melded into a bit of a blob but a reminder of my early service days. Mum said I was a silly sod and Dad said all men in the Army had them. How did he know? Dad never served during the war and maintained he was a "Reserved Occupation". Mum of course said he was a conscientious objector.

I finished the course and was posted to Blandford in Dorset. My troop was nicknamed the "Globe Trotters" (640 Signal Troop) and we were sent out on emergency tours. And I got Shingles. Much to the delight of the camp doctor who I think had never seen it before.

I was glad to be in Blandford as I had recently gained a girlfriend briefly.

The OC of my troop was an arrogant misfit whose father was apparently high up in the army and he (Misfit) obviously thought he was going places. He took an instant dislike to me and when told I was to be forwarded into the high rank of local L/Cpl took the news quite badly. Capt. Misfit could do nothing about it as I was placed in the gymnasium and that post with my course results made him impotent (Not "important"). More about the physical gym work later.

1964 Time for the real stuff as I was on the list for travel and 640 Signal Squadron had my trade skills to unleash elsewhere in the world.

No real trauma except when I had to deliver my Mark 8 Land Rover and my small trailer to our REME mechanics in the camp for its annual inspection. Blandford camp had a circular road running right around the camp. Many years before, motoring clubs would do time trials on a section of the circuit where I was just driving. As the Rover hit a small hilly hump in the road, I heard a loud clunk. Now does anyone remember a show on TV called "THE BIG COUNTRY"? Opening sequence was a horse and buggy crossing a stream with the water splashing on the screen. I won't try to sing this one. Cut a short story long I noticed in my rear-view mirror that my trailer was bounding like a newly born foal in the field to my left. Obviously, I had not checked the split pin, which I should have inserted after attaching the trailer onto the towbar. It looked like slow motion Big Country except no water, just mud flying everywhere. Notwithstanding any damage that may have occurred there was also the condition of the vehicle (how clean it was). I parked up and went into the field to retrieve my trailer. Never won the lottery but this time I had. No damage to the trailer. So quick wipe down. Pin in place and the REME release the vehicle and trailer in a couple of hours with nothing to report.

Just one claim to fame. I was the first Signaller to be issued with the new Mark 8 line laying Land Rover. Love to brag!

All was well and I was on my first leave when a policeman knocked on my mother's front door and I was told to return to camp as the EOKA were causing trouble. EOKA-B was a Greek Cypriot paramilitary organisation. Four of us were sent out. Unbelievably I was on the London Underground with my full battle kit on. Including ammo pouches, a large pack, kitbag, and a suitcase. The passengers were a bit alarmed as we were also carrying our SMGs. (9mm Sterling Machine guns.) Even though the weapons were rolled in hessian the barrels were protruding so no need to guess. Our flight out to Cyprus from an airfield I have since forgotten was in a twin-Engine Eagle Airways plane carrying very few passengers. There was nobody to meet us when we arrived in Nicosia (typical army cock up). We jumped aboard a local bus to Episcopi. Amongst the goats onboard, I wondered how dangerous it was going to be.

Luckily the Paras were also there in force and my tour revolved around cable work and telecom equipment installation. The closest I came to harm was when riding a horse called Meadow Brown in Happy Valley. The horse took off as it saw the stables looming. As we galloped towards the stables MEADOW stopped a football match as she jumped into the netting of the goal but surprisingly did not get caught up. To slow the horses down entering the stables, there were several iron posts just wide enough to get a horse and rider through. I got caught and my shorts were ripped down one side. I never went riding again in Cyprus. The full corporal in charge of us was already based in Cyprus. He was a decent bloke and the only time my best mate Jerry (also from 640) and I had fun with him was on a day we were trying to test a telephone cable which was ducted. We dug down and there we were confronted with two identical earthenware pipes, possibly six inches in diameter. In fairness, nobody could possibly pick which duct contained our cable. What do you think? Corps said to us both. That one, I said, and Jerry looked at me and agreed. The corporal took his pickaxe and attacked the ducting pipe. WOOOSH out spurted gallons of water as Jerry and I burst into laughter.

Blandford beckons after the six-month tour in Cyprus which turned into seven months detachment.

Many years later I was to return to Cyprus with my family for a three-year tour.

Back in Blandford and my girlfriend has gone off with another bloke so saves me some ink here.

Then 640 deemed that I would be of some value by being sent to Aden.

Comms needed the "Brown" touch.
1965 RAF Khormaksa

In the 1960s during operations around Aden/Rhadfan was the busiest ever RAF station. It was overcrowded and the station also attracted terrorist ground attacks. I was Staff Sergeant Gibney's cable jointer and we only worked late afternoons and nights so any telecoms would not be affected by essential installation work. (Others didn't work normally in the afternoon – too hot.) The camp was surrounded by a huge metal fence with the odd double gate. One such gate was about 100 yards from a bungalow which housed the wife of an Admiral (from my recollection). She was asked by some Arabs to open the gate and was threatened verbally. She reported this to the authorities.

In addition to my trade duties, I was still subject to guard duty. My mate Jerry and I were walking the compound. We had to be ten feet apart. It was dark and I thought I saw someone darting through the tumbleweed grounds. I whispered to Jerry and cocked my 7.62 SLR (an overpowered rifle). The first thing was I didn't cock the weapon with any sort of conviction – after all, I had never shot anyone before! The weapon jammed so, as Jerry stood by, I did an unload and reload. This happened again as I saw what I thought was alien motion in the darkness. I said to Jerry I have to pee. He stood by as I found a huge bush which I watered. At that moment a soldier from behind the bush jumped up from the bush. "Why don't you two 'F' off?" An explanation followed. The Sussex Regiment was secretly positioned in the huge compound to defend the Admiral's bungalow should the fence be breached. Another cock up because we as the camp's guard that night had not been told of this plan and had I been more competent may well have resulted in someone being killed. Opposite the Admiral's gate was a volcano which was dormant, and I was told hollow. Later my mate told me there was a pathway under the fence leading to huge doors that gave entrance to this hollowed volcano. There were several huge (44,000 gallons) (hope I got that right) water tanks stuck on top of this dormant, hollow volcano. Later I was told why this place was so important and why it was vital that the entrance on our side of the fence to a tunnel which could be accessed through the Admirals grounds had the highest guarded priority. They called it X-Group. Any guesses? I was told it housed our nuclear bombs in the Middle East. Thinking years later I wondered how sure were they that the volcano was dormant? Especially if there were nuclear explosives stored there. Was I duped? During our morning briefings, the RSM gave situation reports. Grenades were typically thrown over our fence, but the nearest building was well over 100 yards from the perimeter fence so had no effect. The RSM reported bazooka attacks in Mahlar, a town a few miles from the camp. The RSM lived in Mahlar with his wife in a block of flats. He said he would string any Yemeni up, should they be caught! Of course, there were Yemeni spies in the camp who ran the laundry and tailors. The next day a missile went through the next flat to the RSM's quarters. His wife was shipped back to the UK the next day. Just as a matter of interest, the Yemeni didn't realise they had to set the bazooka missiles to explode on impact (I only fired the 84mm twice in all my years in the army so I cannot confirm if the bazooka info was correct at that time.) Consequently the projectile just went through buildings and never exploded.

Next. To catch a thief. Not what you think

I have looked on the internet to find the right name of the Commander in Aden. I thought it was Sir Charles ******** (not surprising I cannot confirm his name, and anyway, I would have been contravening the Official Secrets Act).

Well, Stan my Staff Sergeant boss and I were installing various intercom and telephone systems in the HQ Middle East building. Each day Sir What'shisname stopped for a chat and always ended telling me my watch, which had a luminous dial, would give me cancer due to the radiation from the dial. Having laid the intercom cable from the feed, I entered his office just as he was leaving for the day. At that time, I used to smoke, so having installed and tested the Hadley intercom system and checked the new phone, I sat in his plush chair behind a huge desk. I glanced into his cigar box, poured myself a cognac and started to hum. It was at a time when Robert Wagner was in a TV show called "To Catch a Thief". I always remember the tune. Da, dada da da. Anyway, I glanced around and went to a massive safe embedded in the wall. I went over, hummed the tune and put my hand on the handle...Ah!!! It opened. (Since then, I think he must have left it open.) I panicked, seeing all the documents stamped Top Secret in red. I pressed down on the handle, not realising I was locking an opened door. All the sliders were in lock position. PANIC!!

Only one thing to do. Take off the huge back plate. The sliders which line up to open the door are governed (I think) by the combination. So, when the slider notches line up that is how it should be if the door was opened. Stan came into the office to see how I was getting on. Jesus Christ!!, he said. What have you done.? Fix it!! And off he went mumbling he was never there and knows nothing.

All these sliding bars are on the floor, and I was gradually sliding them back into their slots making sure everything was aligned. Finally, after about an hour, I shut the door and tested it by opening it again without touching the combination dial. All was fine. I shut the door, turned the dial, making sure the safe was locked. It was! Ten minutes wiping all surfaces on the door and dial, and I left to find Stan. We never spoke about it and to this day I wondered if I had truly fixed it. Terrified the door would no longer respond to the correct dialled numbers, I awaited the next day. However, there was no rumbling from HQ Middle East and Stan, and I had finished that project.

We drove back to camp each early morning and for days as we passed the flats lining the street, we always looked up to see a very well-endowed lady naked – at least as far as we could see – waving from her veranda of about seven floors up. We whistled (not politically correct these days but maybe she would agree many years later that she should be a little more modest in attracting us squaddies)!

It was getting near the end of my tour so an afternoon at the Lido (I think at a place called Steamer Point) to have a swim; it was supposed to be relaxing. There was the shark net of course and hundreds of people sunning themselves and swimming. I waded into the water from the hot sand and was immediately stung by a jellyfish. The pain was indescribable, so I won't try. No real respite, just wait until it goes away. Friday came around fast and I was getting excited to return to the UK, just a few more days in this hole. The APL beach was deserted apart from us going-home squaddies. A part of the sea that was free of jellyfish and sharks. We ran around in the surf, shouting and laughing as there were just a few more days to go. Yep! What, no incident? The pain was so bad I knew that I had trod on something hard and needed attention ASAP. Limping out of the surf there was a hole about the size of a ten pence piece in my foot under the arch. Thank you, coral. At the hospital, they were concerned that my arch would fall (whatever that means). I had just the weekend to prove to the doctors that I could walk, otherwise I was not going home soon. The day before flying back I was asked to try to walk. Nothing was going to stop my UK flight. I walked like an Olympian! After the doctor's round, I was granted to fly out the next day. Much of the rest of the time was recovering from my Herculean walk with my foot up and me smiling as if nothing had happened. Stitches still intact. Next, home and waiting for a new posting from the Globe Trotters. In the meantime, do an Assisting Physical Training Course.

I had already completed a "beginner's Fencing course" (not the gardening variety) in 1964 and knew Aldershot PT school. So, on arriving home in late 1965 I side-lined as a secondary trade to become a Physical Training Instructor (not the Army Physical Training Corps). It seemed the only way to gain rank as I was to begin the next 20+ years plus fighting against my superiors. Even after course completion I had to wait as a local L/Cpl for over 11 months before a warrant officer in charge of internal careers found a way to secure "Acting" status, getting more pay for me and eventually substantive rank. A junior ranked soldier, having passed the six-week course in Aldershot, was usually overseen by a Warrant Officer or sometimes a SSgt in the PT Corps who ran the gymnasium within your garrison or regiment.

The course consisted of different disciplines such as Judo, Boxing, Gymnastics, Tug of war, Swimming and more since forgotten, in addition a written paper on Anatomy and physiology. New to me was lesson plans; however, later in my gym career there was a book to aid you in this boring task. Our instructor, whose name was S.Sgt. Keating, was very keen on Tug of War, so we spent a lot of time practising for the inter troop flag competition. We won that discipline and eventually the Flag Competition itself. We all gained yellow belt in Judo following yet another competition. In addition to all the Cross-country running and gym physical tests such as rope climbing and circuit training, I did well in the gymnastics classes as prior to my adult life I was in the Boys Brigade and found a talent for somersaults and falling over.

We had a cross-country race against other troops and as the instructors were in a "Best Troop Competition" amongst themselves but may have been less helpful to those competitors not in their flock. I hate Cross-country and the day of the cross-country race arrived. What made it worse was the PT Instructors were scattered throughout the course to supposedly guide you. BUT, as I was not in one instructors' group, and I was way back in the race, I found myself just before a big metal bridge over a river. I looked at the guide who waved me on. After a few minutes I plodded on to find myself close to a major road or motorway. I turned back and found the bridge which was unmanned. Luckily someone even worse than me at long distance running, had found a path down to the riverbank and at which point he disappeared. I followed and after a short time found myself behind several slow running waifs. There was the end just about half a mile across a large grass field with the instructors eagerly awaiting our return. I tried to make it look like I was spent and developed a rubber leg persona with a head rolling from side to side but as I got closer over around two hundred yards from the end, I sprinted pass two stragglers. My instructor was less impressed even after I relayed my geographic error card which made him even more angry.

We had written exams on the human body and various sporting rules and, finally, some physical contests between the troops. The first one I declined was the gymnastic competition. There was obviously two other men in my troop who lived gymnastics and were better suited for the competition. I restricted myself in the gymnasium under the watchful eye of SSGT Keating to a "Round off back flip and open back somersault" – I don't think he was that impressed. Both our hopefuls failed miserably and to be fair had done better in practice. Now was the time my closest mates and I awaited with some nervous anticipation. The inter troop boxing. There was a lad much taller than I who stood uptight and in training hit the punch bag like George Foreman. Even the instructor was having to lean into the pad as he was exposing the pad to be hit in the various positions presented to mini-George. As time wore on "milling" I believe had the result of several bloody noses. I awaited the now short list of those yet to fight. George's name was shouted out! My mate and I looked at each other. Brown! OMG! To this day I don't know if the staff knew I had boxed as a schoolboy. I thought, try to stay away from that devastating straight left. Funny thing was he seemed less aggressive than I thought he would be. After a couple of tentative straight lefts which I avoided, I threw the odd punch which never actually landed. Suddenly after a brief flurry we went into a clinch. My head was on his chest, his arms were around me except my right arm. I unleased a right hook which I had always been proud of. I didn't see his face as my glove made impact with the left side of his face but instantly I was pulled off by the instructors and "George" was ushered away so quickly I didn't get to say, "Good Fight". My mates were in awe, but I didn't mention my previous experience. We were all back in our troop areas and I never saw my opponent again. The final pass out day and I was looking forward to going back to Blandford and my unit. One last thing to do. Straight to the clothing shop and get my "Crossed Swords", which the tailor on my return sewed to my right upper arm of all my uniforms just above my L/Cpl stripe. I make no apologies as I try to remember so far back, so I stole this list from the internet which I laughingly call memory research, but it does show the mentality and the essential attitude and mindset of physical training instructors of that time and maybe even now.

Famous quotes from PTIs include:

- Ten times round my beautiful body, go!
- No pain – no gain.
- You're in your own time now.
- Pain is weakness leaving the body.
- You call them calves? These are calves!
- Stop whinging... you're supposed to bleed.
- I do this circuit before you're scratching your balls in the morning.
- Just once more round the circuit.
- Breaking into double time.

- That's no hill, just get up it!
- I know a shortcut.
- Press-up position, down.
- Pain is only a sensation and sensations are there to be enjoyed!

Later in my PT mini career I had managed to gain several qualifications. Some that warrant inclusion later in the book. What I didn't realise was that these courses were the steppingstone to my Sgt rank. Some of the courses were: Freefall Parachutist; Special Expedition Leader; Canoeing Instructor; fencing for beginners (Not DIY); Basic Rock climbing, liked the views! Unit first aid Instructor; and finally Nuclear and Biological Instructor (lapsed).

In 1966 I met a girl from Fenham near Newcastle. She was a military telephone operator. We met when I was seconded to the National Rifle Association during the Canadian Shooting Championship. Anyway, it was a short job and to some extent a bit of a holiday. My job was to set out the field telephones at each distance where the firing trenches were in the event of possible accidents. During the days when there was no shooting, I was asked to man the small telephone exchange. After the odd complaint a real operator was found due to my complete incompetence. Helen was a lovely girl. I only mentioned Helen as it led to an event I wish to forget but have been unable to do, even though it was so many years ago. We will come to that. Well into our mini-courtship I was forced to return to Blandford after the completion of my short secondment and was met with some devastating news. I was about to go to a little paradise in the Indian Ocean 20 degrees south of the Equator. The Maldives! Gan Island, situated in the Addu Atoll 540km south of the capital Male, in the Indian Ocean. It was to be both epic and a glitch in any thoughts of promotion above the now heady heights of my current rank of Lance Corporal, only previously gained as a local physical training instructor. The posting also led to the partial demise of my relationship with Helen.

The VC 10 circled to land on the 3000 by 2000-yard island. The island was beautiful. At the base of a horseshoe atoll. I was met by an old friend whose name escapes me, but he had a broken front tooth; we had a small amount of history drinking. It was very early in the morning. He explained the island was a staging post for transportation to Singapore. The Royal Signals man in charge of maintaining the telephone and other equipment on Gan was a Staff Sergeant named Ron Knight. I was to meet staff later that morning for the do's and don'ts introduction. I was to replace the only cable jointer, a full corporal due to fly home after completing his one-year tour. During the introduction, I made a poor impression as Ron suggested I could make full corporal if I worked hard. Blah, blah, blah. I was 21, away from my new love for a year. Straight away I said I didn't need a carrot and I was on Gan to do the job which I was very good at and that is what I intend to do. BAD MOVE. At that instant, Ron had me down as a rebellious little upstart. I found my eight-man room housed in the Royal Airforce Police block with a veranda. My newfound other workmates, a total of eight including another Staff Sergeant, a Foreman of Signals technician in charge of the Strowger exchange, who made me welcome. The boys as normal took me out that night. The object of this social event was to find out whose camp I was in socially. Was I to be a saver (hermit), or an occasional drinker, or a lush? I was set on being the occasional drinker as I was fixed on marrying Helen. BUT! I was going to show the boys I was in the top bracket of drinkers on this initiation night. As a very young reader of things like Coral Island and seeing the film Robinson Crusoe, I wondered what would happen if the castaway had a medical emergency. I guessed that you were to have perhaps a painful end after your appendix ruptured. Anyway, off we went. I was drinking lager and Brandy and Blackcurrant as a chaser. These boys were good, and the night ended with me giggling and falling onto my back in front of the veranda just short of my bed. Of course, I was left there. After all, I would wake up and make it to my pit (bed). I did wake up as the rain came down like a monsoon. Frogs jumping over my torso. I stood up and promptly discharged much of what I had eaten the night before. The stomach pain was quite like something I had before, at Aldershot hospital being deemed to be food poisoning. Early Saturday morning, I was down to the medical centre as things were getting quite serious. That evening I was visited by the doctor as I lay in bed in the hospital. I was awoken as the Flight Sergeant seemed to think I was in some distress but funnily I thought I was having a good sleep. Pushing down on my stomach a couple of times the doc continued to depress my stomach. I threatened the doc not to do it again as I was likely to punch his lights out, and he said you have appendicitis. Midnight I was prepped (shaving etc) and that was it.

Everyone that I know who had spent time in army hospital had the perverse objective in trying to make you laugh post-operation. Sounds rather primitive now, but the idea was to see whose stitches would burst first. Two days went by, and I was visited by my new comrades who said Ron was not amused. Worse! He also was in the hospital with an unknown-to-me ailment. As we all laughed at our stupid jokes, an orderly arrived at my bedside saying, Staff Knight asked how I had felt on my admission and that he was not well and all he could hear in the next ward was my stupid laughter. Finally, we were both discharged and after the stitches were taken out, I visited the tailors to collect my Air Formation overseas wear. Ron said he needed confirmation of my L/Cpl promotion, so I was not allowed my stripe. The day started with an angry statement from Ron about my attitude, telling me to report to the telephone exchange. The centre of Gan Island was below sea level and the cable pit in the exchange used to fill up, especially following a rainstorm. Much of my first working day on the island was spent bailing out the cable pit with a bucket. Eventually, after several days confirmation came through and up went the stripe, much to Ron's disgust.

Willey Suckling was a new mate and both of us were interested in archery. There was the Airforce Archery Champion who ran the Archery club (total membership, HIM!). We joined and I sent away for an Apollo Martin bow with a set of steel arrows. Our practising was done alongside the runway, usually at 100 yards subject to Air Traffic Control permission. Nobody was hurt.

Now the blunders were to me quite funny in my opinion. But Ron was near despair with my infectious antics. I now had troop allies.

The "Wave Victor" was a large oil containership permanently anchored just offshore. The ship was the top-up fuelling station for the aircraft on Gan. At a certain time of the year, we connected a cable to the ship from the land while the ship itself was topped up with aviation fuel. We were able to get the cable installed by using a small skiff with an outboard motor to get our telephone cable connected to the ship. The temporary cable was installed for comms between the ship and land as the "Wave Victor" was itself refuelled by a supply ship. On completion, without any event, we headed back to our little buoy and tied up to the bobbing orange ball. What we didn't realise was the tide was low. (Not really a tide on Gan, to be fair.) It was called High and Low water. So, Low water. That night (not Ron) the monsoon-like rain poured down so no going out. Next after a warm maintenance working day, we boys set out to have a boat day with Ron's permission. We arrived at our little buoy to find a sunken boat. Securely tied in the Low tide position so when the high water arrived the water just poured into the boat. We realised then that we were not always playing with a full deck. Sensibility took over and we bailed out the little skiff so as not to break its back by trying to initially turn it over. Clever, eh? How Ron found out I don't know, but to my surprise, he was not too angry until the day the engine was due to be serviced by the Marine Section and I was holding the rope being used to raise the engine onto the jetty. We were at low water so a 12-foot drop to the surface of the water. Part way up the lift, the rope started to slip through my hands. The burning sensation was not wasted on me, and I promptly let go. Down into the depths went the entire engine. Ron was quite vexed, especially as I was the only one in the troop that could free dive to get a new rope attached. He probably thought well, it was going in for service anyway, plus I think I was wearing him down.

Noddy was one of two monkeys that had jumped a ship passing Gan. One died later; Noddy survived. This evil monkey had been trained by some pervert to masturbate while sitting on the desk in the arrivals' hall. Gan was a staging and refuelling base, so wives and loved ones travelling to Singapore would deboard during refuelling by waiting in the arrival hall. During the initial hand performance, Noddy would Nod as he was satisfying himself (hence his name) and followed this by jumping on any unsuspected traveller's shoulders and tweaked that person's nipples. I am an animal lover, but I really wanted to kill that annoying primate. There were some funny things I remember to this day (obviously) that I need to pass on when they occur to me.

On certain evenings we would go to the pictures and queued to buy a spam roll and an orange drink at the mobile van. We selected our seats to watch the trailers. My first time was hilarious. Do those of my generation remember the Rothman's King Size Cigarette advert? The advert said, "Rothmans, King Size", (there was a pause) "King size cigarettes". So, I am sat there, and the advert came on. Rothman's King size cigarettes at which point the whole audience shouted out WHAT SIZE? King size the commentary continued. As if answering. I creased up! Such things like that happened all the time. I began to realise these guys had been on an all-male island for many months and needed some amusement. I say all male but there was one woman, a weever (WVS) – I forgot to mention her. Her name was Roddy and she brought around books for us to read in hospital. I think she was in her 40s. Each day walking around the hospital wards she would ask the same question with a twinkle in her eye. "Can I do anything for you boys? **Apart from that**!!"

The months wore on and I was still writing to Helen and sending a recorded tape to my parents. At the six-month point you could opt to go home for a week; the other option was to go to Singapore. You can guess, can't you. I had originally been to Dover Road Camp (not Air Formation) in Singapore en route to Gan Island. I chose to go oriental. I stayed in a camp in Changi. Some might remember the film with Steve Mc Queen, called "King Rat" filmed in Changi Jail. The machine gun posts on the corner of the jail towers were still used. As usual the guys took you downtown to chat up the women. Bugis Street had the best-looking women. Many had perfect figures and wore tightfitting and sometimes sequined dresses. Only problem was: they were not women! Eventually I ended up in the New Zealand Bar. Her name was Lilian Lee, she lived at 252 Tiong Bahru Rd. Singapore 3. Might not have the correct spelling. One day while waiting for her to start work in the New Zealand Bar, I sat in the high-backed wooden churchlike booth. The seats were back-to-back so if the person on the other side jumped back you were forced forward as it was a complete unit. The Vietnam war was raging, and the fleet was in. Four big American sailors came in. Those silly Popeye hats had me annoyed instantly. As they sat down the seat moved and my drink nearly fell out of my hand. What the "F" I said. At which point the heads came over the top and looked at the insignificant Brit. They must have thought I wasn't worth bothering with (and looking back I was pleased). Time wore on and the Popeyes were getting smashed, and I was irritated to find out Lilian wasn't working that day. Suddenly, the Popeyes lost it, and glasses were hitting the tiled walls. The owner must have had a hotline to the shore patrol. I have never seen such huge men with white batons come into a bar ready to clean up. I sobered up in an instant and produced my Brit ID in a nanosecond. The patrol gushed in like a tsunami and they just started swinging. Only one word to describe it: "Carnage". In no seconds flat they were carrying out the unconscious and bodily able Popeyes and thinking back I don't think they gave any warning or questioned the rowdies. The bar owner smiled, and I bought another drink and booked a taxi. Changi village had a great restaurant that did mushroom egg omelettes.

Lilian was from Penang, so I took her to the beach. We also went to Tiger Palm Gardens and again I nearly ended up in fight with a stallholder on the walking pathway to the Gardens. He was saying something about her being a Bar Girl. I caught on and she dragged me away, saying it didn't matter. I lost the info on who had these gardens built in honour of his wife, but he must have been influential. Having said that, if you ever get to go there, if it is still there, you might want to NOT take your kids. Much of it was characters in some form of torture. Disembowelling, feet in hot lead and more. You get the picture. Finally, it was time to fly back to Gan. I bid Lilian goodbye who I don't think was that sad as she probably moved on to another customer.

We taxied onto the runway and then taxied back onto the pan. We waited in our seats. We taxied out again and back again. Apparently, the plane had a fuel pump problem, and it would take another ten days to get the replacement. Ah! Sad! I stayed in Changi as I had run out of money and just pottered around the village. Not 100 percent truthful there! My RAF mate, also from Gan, had money, and he said he would take me out for one last blast. All went well even when we got into one of the famous petrol station taxis. These taxis transported you to a porn movie or the real thing and back. My air force buddy said he would pay for it all but needed the company – and of course just in case things went tits up, as he put it.

The movie show was in a small breezeblock square about 20 by ten feet and the film was shot onto part of the wall which was whitewashed to look like a screen. No roof of course. Following a couple of movies, we were a little bit bigger in the trouser department. Back to our original taxi and our driver sat there knowing where the next stop would be. After a short drive we were ushered into a small room leading off to a corridor, which later I found led to several bedrooms. Six girls of various sizes and nationalities stood grinning at us. Sat on a sofa with a free beer, we were to pick who we wanted. If your gaze fell on one for maybe five seconds, she would appear behind you laughing and running her fingers through your hair. Ok, off we go. I entered the room and my selection jumped onto the bed. I folded up my trousers as she smiled. Eventually all was set. Just one thing I said, "Can we turn the light out?" She nodded but asked for the 15 dollars first. Thanks, mate. I had put the money in my back pocket and for some reason (I don't know if this has happened to anyone else) I couldn't find the notes. They were so close to the lining of my pocket, and I struggled to feel the paper money. After about ten seconds she shouted, at which point a man came crashing into the room just as the outside of my fingers brushed against paper, phew! She waved him out and after I asked if she was clean, she nodded, she turned the light out just as I was jumping onto the bed. OOPS, in the darkness I had managed to elbow her in her eye. She screamed, the light went on and hey! You're back again! The man was not pleased but luckily the girl explained it had been an accident. I was on my second time around, but she caught on and slid out of bed to find the light switch. She passed me a tissue and told me to put it in the bucket, which was half full; I just hoped that it was filled over a week of trading, but I doubted it. I bid her farewell and waited in the taxi for my mate to come out. The taxi driver was making a mint out of my mate. He jumped in and related his girl's passing goodbye in which she had said he was very good. Bragger! I didn't pass on my antics. In fact, this has been the first time since 1966 that I have admitted having been to a brothel and glad to say, never have been since. The VC10 flight back to Gan was uneventful with our replacement fuel pump working marvellously. One quick mention of our laundry man and the bedroom cleaner. Mohamad Futta, who used to row from his island to Gan each day, and Abdul who I believe walked across the causeway. Poor men but hard working, and in the case of Mohamad was a class act.

As was usual in the military during Christmas we lesser ranks were served Christmas dinner by the Senior NCOs and Officers. A lot of soup was spilt as the high-class waiters had already had a skinful in their respective messes.

Christmas time on Gan was magical. Each section could make a bar and sell the booze with the Station Commander's blessing. The imagination of some of the sections was exceptional, one was a Mississippi Steamboat, another a Cave and so many more. There were only us eight Signallers and two Postal Royal Engineers, the rest Brylcreem boys. In those days the Brylcreem boys were "RAF" as they seem to slick their hair down with that cream. The Corporal Postie called everyone "Doris". He said he was terrible with names so called everyone Doris and get this… "So as not to offend those whose names he had forgotten." Ha! Ha!

Trying to keep fit I played a lot of badminton and rugby on Gan and on occasion practised a bit of gymnastics. I met a huge RAF policeman called Dick Grinnell. Dick had trained with a guy called Steve Reeves, who I believe was a film star. I only saw one of his films called "Hercules Unchained". Dick said he had a great body but was as weak as a kitten. During a visit from a Royal Navy Ship en route to Singapore, we played the minesweeper crew at rugby. They beat us by a gazillion points. Apparently, they trained by running around the ship all day.

Well, time for a night out with the Matlows. "Apparently from the French name for 'sailor' (Matelot)." We walked/staggered our newfound drinking buddies to the jetty to catch the last liberty boat back to their ship. It was low water. A sort of long rowing boat appeared, except it was powered by an outboard motor. Those that didn't make it to the water taxi were going to the brig in the morning. The shore patrol arrived as we managed to get those conscious back to the jetty as things would start to get uncomfortable for those who had decided to lie down or who fell sleep on the raised ledge from the 12-foot fall to the water. Yes, it was the infamous low water. The bodies were lined up, and as the liberty boat slowly chugged by then two shore patrol policemen just gently pushed the bodies off the jetty. Many were lucky and avoided the bench seats in the boat, but the odd one must have wondered how he had sustained broken ribs. Hey! I was okay when I left the bar.

Everyone was beside themselves with excitement. The Rusty E was coming to Gan. On its last trip. HMS Eagle was paying a visit en route to Singapore. The old carrier hosted us, and we were given a tour inside the living quarters and of course the huge hangar where there were several aircraft. Six-foot tables were set out in a big square. Inside the square were several dustbins. Each dustbin was full of beer and several sailors dunked glasses to the brim, handing the glass to us as we passed by towards a finger buffet. (Not real fingers, just sandwiches and stuff on cocktail sticks.) Come to think of it, I didn't see anyone ask for a Gin and Tonic and there were dozens of Officers forming dinner-party like groups. Having found new friends, we were shown their living quarters. Why is it – or is it just me? – that wonders why these huge ships have such small living areas for the crew to sleep in? Six men in two tiers of three bunk beds. Showing sympathy to the men, I said, "Why haven't they at least sorted out the ceiling where the panels were hanging down?" "Oh," said one rating. "That is us! That is where we hide cigarettes, booze etc when we come into port back in Blighty." Apparently, it was the custom! Or something about the customs. Me being a bit dim. PS You didn't hear this from me.

My Akai played Johnny Mathis and I thought about Helen. I glanced at my crib going home wallchart. There was a long crazy pathing path winding to the front door leading from Gan. Each day a stone was coloured in, and the home front door signified when I had set foot back in Blighty. Ron's tour was over, and we were to get an Electrician Driver, a Staff Sergeant to oversee us. Ron wrote a scathing report on me as it was his duty to provide "constructive" assessments of his men for their future promotion. In my case "destructive" I guess – if he had his way I would be demoted. (Years later when I was the Deputy Group Supervisor at Line Group in 8 Signal Regiment Trade Training School, I was tasked as the Sergeant's Mess Entertainments man to host a group of officers visiting 8 Signal Regiment. The RSM introduced me to the officer I was to host. Yes, it was Major Ron Knight. We sat at the bar, and he said, "You could have gone far." "Nah!" I said, "I was a prat." He didn't object to the statement but just smiled into his drink. Ron, like so many of my comrades or in Ron's case an acquaintance, have since passed. I have realised I am incapable of sympathy when it comes to death. At least today reviewing my scribble. Years later, my ex-son in law was telling me about how he had lost his father a few months prior. I said," That was careless." Not long now Brown, I keep saying. As I am an agnostic, I hope I am right because there are some I would rather not meet again. Talking of being an agnostic/atheist, this appeared on my Facebook page. So, here it is: - Any such reader may well tear up this book, burn it and make a small doll effigy of me to stick pins into. What follows is just thought provoking. Please don't be offended if you are not scientifically motivated.

I do believe that millions in this world need a belief of an afterlife. I hope not after seeing what a mess we are making of this one.

THE STORY OF GOD (Cut and pasted from my file of useless Facebook friends.)

God had no beginning. He was always there. He is maximally intelligent. We don't exactly know what this means but let's say his IQ is a few billion compared to our average IQ of 100.

And he was alone. Definitely. We are told he is the ONLY real god – all the others are human inventions. So, he had no friends, no wives, no one to talk to, nothing to do, no TV, no Internet, no nothing. He didn't even have day and night. As far as we know, he spent infinitely long in pitch dark and terrible cold all alone. But he must have been happy because he is perfect.

At some point he tired of being alone and decided to make some friends to love. He made an unimaginably huge universe and then made trillions of solar systems and in one he placed a tiny (and rather dangerous) planet for his friends to live on. He looked at his creation and thought it was good. (Turns out it wasn't.)

With preparations done, he created his new friends. Now, you might think he would have made them as intelligent as himself. That would have allowed for interesting late-night conversations. He could even play games with them and not always win. But he didn't. He made his friends pitifully weak; very, very tiny, belligerent, argumentative and very, very, very stupid (compared to himself).

Well, they say God works in mysterious ways, but this was like a lonely human being making bacteria for company. Unsurprisingly, it didn't work out too well.

He was careful to provide each human with a dedicated comms channel, so he could talk to each one directly. Yet still many of them didn't love him back, some didn't even believe he existed! He wanted them to follow his rules of behaviour but most of them ignored him. They even invented their own gods, and some masturbated!

Finally, he was so exasperated with his friends that he decided to kill them all. What else could he do? He truly loved them, but they ignored him. He just left one family alive whom he thought would behave better. I suppose we could call this supernatural selection!

Well, to cut a long story short, it still didn't work out. Humans continued to do their own thing; some of them pretended to love him, some of them loved other gods and hardly any of them would stone their unruly sons to death.

God was at his wits' end. So, he thought, and he thought (with an IQ of several billion, that's a heck of a lot of thought) and came up with his master plan. He would come to Earth as a human and have the locals kill him as a sacrifice to himself. Then he would be able to forgive all past, present, and future human sin; obviously. What could possibly go wrong?

Of course, it is possible that this story is not true. We can either believe that the immensely powerful being with a several billion IQ did all this, or we can believe the whole story was invented by tiny, tiny beings who are very, very, very stupid (compared to God). I don't know. What do you think?

Back to Gan. Oh, I forgot. Ron was nearly killed. He was a useless swimmer but had all the gear. Knife strapped to his leg, snorkel, mask, and a spear gun. Now I was not there but I saw the photo. We had some nasty stuff in our waters around Gan and at that time no antidote to a Stone Fish Sting. No, he didn't, pity. Anyway, he was apparently plodding along looking into little caves in the coral reef when out came a Moray eel at some pace. Morays are very dangerous, especially in defence. Apparently, Ron was startled and let fly (more from panic I was told) and the spear from the gun went through the eye of the Moray. Anywhere else and Ron would have been bitten and possibly maimed because this eel was big. I don't know the circumference of the eel, but it looked from a flat view on the photo as about eight inches across. Ron was 5ft 8 in and he was holding up the eel still impaled on the spear and the eel's tail was just touching the floor and its head level with Ron's (head that is, because Ron didn't have a tail). Hard to tell them apart really.

My new boss Staff Sergeant Jacobs was given quite a big project to do, and it involved a 254 pair paper insulated lead cable. At a time when the cable sleeve covering the joint was not sealed using the epoxy putty type, or heat shrink type later introduced, I had to deal with the expanding joint closure. (Bloody useless system.) I decide to fill the sleeve with wax because it would be monsoon time soon and a bit wet. When we tested the cable, it had one pair faulty. I think the hot wax had burnt through the paper insulation on that pair and caused a short. Yep! I jointed the whole thing again. Late into the afternoon as I was finishing up, having now tested the cable as 100 percent, I was soldering the sleeve nozzle used in pouring in the bees' wax, when my new boss appeared. I told him what had happened, and he said one pair faulty would have been acceptable. Well done anyway! Who was this man? I was touched. A compliment from a boss! When the reporting time came again my write up was excellent. He said in my interview, "I tried to overwrite the past year's assessment as it didn't reflect a true assessment of you." He hoped it would offset my previous assessment. The great day arrived. The flight home filled me with mixed feelings, plus I wouldn't miss the bats flying out of the trees as we came out of the cinema. They had a habit of urinating on us as they took off from the trees.

1967: Helen met me at the railway station; she had put on a little weight. Her friends all said, she never once went out on the town whilst I was away. I felt guilty and questioned what I would do when I had spent some time at home. Helen's father was a scout for a third division football team. I mentioned him because he was the one who suggested we wait in getting engaged before I went to Gan. After a family visit, a painful separation occurred (my mother and auntie adored her). Helen was in tears on the telephone at the exchange in Aldershot. I ended our relationship as I was now about to be thrown in at the deep end, physically, emotionally and in the promotion stakes. Things took a turn to the below average. To this day I think of Helen as a kind, loving young woman who I had treated badly. I hope she has since had a GOOD HAPPY LIFE. xx

Mum and Dad had retired and moved to Plymstock in Devon to be nearer to Aunt Fay in Plymouth. Mum had developed cancer. Again, I will try to recall in sequence the events leading up to her death.

I was in Catterick, again. This time I was at 11 Sig Regt employed in the training wing. Back in the Gymnasium, training recruits. My base was "Le Chateau Gym" (long since demolished). My boss was a Warrant Officer called Ken Norris from Liverpool whose saying was, "You Big Girl's Blouse". At that time I was a fair swimmer and gained my Amateur Swimming Association Examiner's award and Royal Life Saving Teacher's Award. Bragging again! We, my new ex-para-Sigs mate "Big bad Stan" as a pair, won several little cups and medals especially for the lifesaving events and relays. Big bad Stan was from Batley. Quite tall, stocky, barrel chested and a slight rebel, this ex-216 Para Signals Lance Corporal took no nonsense. Stan suited me down to the ground as a work and social mate. Jane, his wife, was a looker, they had a small child; whereas I was working at it, getting a wife I mean. Other instructors in the Gym were a Scouse whose last name was Drennan, obviously from Liverpool. Another called Frank Moodie, a Catholic from Glasgow. Eddie Fitch, whose wife had died and left him with two young children. Ricky Broad who had a twin, not in the Army – his twin and I met in Wales in a pub when I was climbing. I thought it was Rick, home on leave as he had progressed into the Army PT

Corps having been on a Para course saying it was the hardest work he had done since joining the army. His twin was not as interesting as Rick, so I drank up and unhooked. Just to explain that. The pub had a rock-faced wall with belays (places to clip your carabiner onto to stay safe). I was on the lower part of the rock as I wanted to be closer to the bar. I mentioned Catholic with regards to Frank because it became a problem for him as his wife was a Protestant, but eventually all was sorted out.

Ken called me into the office and said a high up officer was visiting and I was to take the recruit class. I was to submit a "Lesson Plan" and allocate jobs to the other instructors for the lesson. The Officer arrived and I briefed the recruit class. "You are being watched by a very high ranked officer from the Army Physical Corps, so work hard."

Everyone including my fellow instructors pushed the recruits as they negotiated around the circuit course. I could not have made a better impression on my superiors. Within a week I was promoted to full Corporal.

LCpl Frank Moodie, however, was quite bitter when I got my second stripe. Tough!

There used to be an army nightclub of sorts called the Harewood Club. Some of us PTIs went out for a beer or two and I was the last to leave as the others set off for the fish and chip shop. As I came out of the club, four of my recruits rushed up saying there were four others wanting to fight. (Tank Regiment and Signals usually ending up in a brawl during the 60s for some unknown vendetta). In a moment they appeared. They accused my guys of chatting up their girls or some such nonsense. The gobby one was the smallest. I said rubbish, these guys had been with me all night. Gobby tried to brush me aside, at which point

I pushed him back about four yards with a force I don't think he was prepared for. Gobby ran at me. I performed quite the best non-punching action I could take. The judo move I performed was Tsuri goshi (hip throw). Now in the dojo you always hung onto the opponent's sleeve, so I did bang my own elbow on the pavement. Eventually as I sat on his shoulders I gave him a bloody nose and kneed him over a small hedge; he was out of it, so I approached the other three. By this time, our remaining enemy were clenching fists. Listen, I said, we don't want trouble, so we are just going back to camp. We started to walk, and the bully boys went to help their dwarf. I was taller by a clear inch. The next day in the Gym the troop were saying thanks again and how impressed they were. I told them to shut up and get into the gym. I was getting a bit of a reputation which I did not want. Plus, Ken would have gone nuts if he had caught wind of what I did. Frank had been in the chip shop as our four advisories came in. Gobby was saying he thought I was a martial arts expert. At that time some would have said "Piss Artist expert". Frank knew by the conversation that I had been involved. No more fighting until we get to America in another book attempt, where I took up Taekwondo, for a little while. Also featuring two more marriages making four in total. Can't wait, can you?

Back to the gym. The day came, training recruits in the indoor swimming pool so they could pass their recruit swimming test. The pool was contained within a building called Sandy's, a building now housing some Headquarters pen pushers. Which also had a café and other facilities. Now, I had noticed one man whose course I oversaw. There is a thing called the Standing Jump. You stand side on and jump to the highest you can and tip the top of the wall with your fingers. This gorilla jumped above the recording board. He was also incredibly strong. We will call him Guy, after the since-gone gorilla in London Zoo. Guy swam like a lead balloon. Two strokes in, across the width of the small pool he started to thrash about. I was looking elsewhere as we had quite a few men in the pool. Ken, the boss, shouted to me. I dived in and breast stroked towards Guy. Classic, talking calmly trying to get him to put his hands on my shoulders facing me and lie back. Then I could breaststroke him to the edge of the pool, just about three metres. No chance, he grabbed me in a wrestler's grip around my whole body. He would not let me get him into the clasping chin position and seemed to think all would be well by dragging me down or thinking I was a float. Training tells you to get under water if all the other reactions like palming him off on the chin and other preventative reactions did not work with the panic stricken, thrashing person. I sank intentionally. He would let go as he tried to stay above the waterline. He did. I went to the bottom of the pool as I had the ability to hold my breath for some time. I stood on the bottom put my hands under his butt and lifted him and walked carrying him like that underwater to the edge of the pool. He was so grateful. I explained to Guy what I had tried to do and later he understood that nobody on our watch was going to drown. Later, he did pass the width test mainly by thrashing his arms about, causing a tidal wave and through brute force and panic.

We had the weekly wash up in front of Ken. Stood in a line awaiting the question from him, Why didn't you! Previously that week I was lead instructor, running my troop over the assault course. I swear if I was in the situation I found myself in, I would never do what I did ever again. The men had run over the course really without incident so I stupidly decided they could run the reverse and then we would finish. The water jump had a straight concrete edge leading to the slanted landing spot. In jumping the opposite way around, the jumper was landing on good land or would hit the right-angled concrete edge. There was a scream as one recruit didn't make good land. This young man had hit the right angle of the concrete and was dragged out of the water by me and two recruits. I lifted his trouser leg to find a huge cut to his shin. I detailed two men to carry him to the Medical Centre. Curiously, none of these traumatic events came to the attention of higher authorities.

So, what was I in for? You! he said, pointing at me. That lad on the top of the net on the assault course, why didn't you leave him there? If it had been me I would have done so, said Ken. He went on to say, "I would have backed you. You'd have backed me if our roles were reversed, wouldn't you?" I couldn't stop myself. I said, Would I F…. There was a brief taking in of the breath and snigger by my comrades as I followed this by a quick explanation. Hell, if we had left him at the top of the 12ft net in the terrified state he was in, he may well have fallen off with nobody around to pick up the pieces. Legally we wouldn't have had a leg to stand on. Surprise!! Ken nodded.

Summertime, we in the gym did lifesaving duties at the newly opened open air swimming pool down Shute Road, camp centre, and, during the winter we ran a Judo Club in the gym on a Tuesday evening. Being professional, I didn't take much notice of the girls and not knowing I had met my wife-to-be. We stayed together for nearly 19 years. Outside the old YMCA was where I eventually spoke to her. She was in her friend's truck, and I recognised her, but this time she was wearing makeup. We had a brief kiss and arranged a proper date.

A bit about my ex-wife. As time wears on regarding our relationship, in retrospect, I think we were equally to blame for the eventual divorce so many years later. Jennifer, although only 17 but nearly 18, was more sexually experienced than I, not in the act but with how many, if you catch my drift.

Jennifer had a brother and sister who were twins; they were youngest of four kids to Mr and Mrs Carver. The eldest daughter was Pam, a schoolteacher. We were not the best of friends from the start.

I cannot remember our first date. But I do remember a grope in a bus shelter and later in a shunter's hut by the railway line close to her home in Colburn. Jennifer never bragged, but unknown to me she worked in the Admin Office in our regiment. It turned out she was a Clerical Officer. Jennifer's father quite liked me but as you can tell at that time, I was not the brightest candle in the holder. So, the father first.

Cecil Carver was a tech civilian instructor at 8 Sigs trade training regiment, teaching technicians both at an entry level and on upgrader courses. He had served in the Signals during the war. Lieutenant Carver was also at Dunkirk. Eventually we played a lot of golf, usually at Catterick Golf course. He had a little Jack Russell called Judy. Cecil trained Judy to hunt for balls that were only in the rough. He was the only person allowed on the course with a dog. Everyone knew Judy, she was a wonderful little dog. This was a little income for Cecil who then sold the balls on to the club professional who used them for his practice students. One day I had been slicing balls everywhere and each time, Cecil said to me, try this. So, by the 17th, which drives past the clubhouse, I was fuming!! I put my left foot forward, turned the club in my hand and all those things to cure the slice.

I hit the ball with some venom. It took off at about a foot high and bent like John Inman. At 90 degrees turning left straight through one of the several small windows of the outer door to the clubhouse. Onwards, straight through the inner glass door window and hit the bar. Cecil said, "You better see what's what." I entered the clubhouse bar and all heads turned. At the bar a man was holding my ball. "This yours?" he said. I bowed my head and nodded. It turned out nobody was injured but he, the holder, was the club treasurer. He charged me a guinea for the window replacement, and all was forgiven.

Most of the Carvers were tall except Val, one of the twins. She was about 5 ft 4 ins tall. Cecil was about 6ft 1 inch, Phil the other twin eventually topped out about the same. Jennifer was about 5ft 7ins tall. The only noticeable thing about Jennifer was her slightly lazy eye which she later tried to have fixed but gave up after the initial operation failed.

More later about Jennifer to almost present day. Then back to my life experience with her in sequence. After our divorce, Jennifer had become a nurse and joined the Reserve Army, getting a commission. Later she got her degree and then onto her masters and received some medals as lead nurse during the Iraq war. Jennifer retired as a Major I believe. I have never asked. At this very moment in time, she is in Turkey with my girls, celebrating Tracey's 50th and in three days' time my other daughter's 51st birthday – that would be Karen.

Back to our lead up to marriage. It will come as no surprise that Jennifer became pregnant. I arranged a registry wedding at Richmond in Yorkshire. I was concerned in what fighting tactic I would need when Cecil found out. But the mother told him and things turned out alright.

All the boys from the gym and I met in one of the dozens of pubs in Richmond, North Yorkshire just a hundred yards from the Registry Office. Cecil was waiting outside as I trotted around the corner. All was well and the short ceremony was over in about 15 minutes. Cecil decided not to party with us so went home with his wife Mary to their house in Constantine Ave in Colburn. It was Jennifer's 18-year birthday, 30th November 1968.

Funny thing is I don't remember much about the remainder of the day. Jennifer was to live at her parents' house as normal until I could get a married quarter. Now here is a little about Army bureaucracy. There was always a waiting list for quarters. You had points gained for various reasons. Obviously how long you had been waiting, your rank and extenuating reasons. I badgered the Housing Officer who was a Sergeant near the end of his service who had a thankless job designating quarters. There were several bungalows, back-to-back type residences which nobody wanted. I was offered one in fact. The Housing Officer said there was nothing else. Late afternoon I had managed to get time off to once again see the housing officer. I took Jennifer, who was clearly pregnant. Jennifer sat there; head bowed with her hands clasped. The Housing officer was ill at ease, so I tried the old "We have nothing" ploy. I said, you want my wife to maintain two bungalows that are empty in the condition she is in. The poor man was near to tears which prompted my wife to sob quietly and that did it. "We do have a portacabin quarter in Marne Lines." These quarters were just a mile from my camp. We did not hesitate in accepting. We moved in immediately and then I realised that although you got all the kitchenware and bedding etc, there were other things that couples needed.

I was in the corporal's mess at Naafi break. I put my last sixpence in the slot machine and WOW! I won the jackpot: £5.00. Of course, the rest of the guys said, Drinks all round! I ignored them all and after work went to the local wholesalers and put the £5.00 down on a vacuum cleaner.

Joe, our black PT Instructor, a L/Cpl, lived next door and his wife was also pregnant. Later, after she had given birth to the child, she rejected it because they had to pull the child out with a plunger so the child had a misshapen head; later this gradually returned to the normal shape you would expect. During this time Jennifer mentored her and eventually things panned out.

I spent some time in making a clothes horse. It was relatively successful but far from professional and Jen never commented on its design. We had our new Hoover. Becoming affluent.

The first inkling of Jen and her possible questionable loyalty and ethics became apparent when one night I was on guard duty, and she, and Pam her sister, had a girl's night out. It was around midnight; I was on guard duty. I popped home leaving the 2 i/c in command. I'll only be half an hour I said. I walked in the front door and Jennifer came out of the bedroom. I can't remember how it arose, but she said, DON'T go in there. To this day I don't know why I obeyed and said I will be home at eight o'clock in the morning. The subject never came up and to this day the forceful way she said it implied to me there was a man or men in the bedroom with her and her sister.

To become a Sergeant, you had to have a First-Class Cert in education and in trade. Unknown to me the education issue caused a delay of many years to my promotion. In those days there was a host of subjects you could choose from, to get your First-Class Ed. You had to have Maths, English and any other two subjects. World and Current Affairs was another encouraged topic to master. My father-in-law knew the lecturer at 1 AEC (Education centre in Catterick). According to my father-in-law it was unlikely that I would pass the Physics course as outlined by my teacher.

However, everybody underestimated me. I passed all the exams including the Physics paper. I was qualified educationally for promotion. For over eight years I had stagnated because I was not qualified for promotion. The rules had changed in the November and only set subjects such as Maths, English, Current affairs, and Army Organisation gave you the qualification. I screamed on the phone when a records clerk said I did not have my Ace 1 in education. I said, I did, and I had gained the full qualification BEFORE the November of that year before the rules changed. The Clerk checked back and then said oh! Yes. Congratulations you have your ACE one. Right! Eight bloody years too late. Within two days my certificate arrived but any chance of promotion immediately now depended on my annual write up and we all know how those go.

Some Gymnasium stuff. Many years before my so-called academic army education, I was really into sports. As I have said before, much of my recordings here just jump out to me as something I should have mentioned in actual order but may not be in correct sequence to the actual events. (Did I mention the parachuting? I'll check.) Anyway, I was in Aldershot and managed to get into the semi-final of the Corps Badminton Championships. Although I was in the Corps team, it was the only time I was really interested in trying to maintain some sort of national prowess. Next was my Army Football referee award and later as an Army Rugby Coach.

Back home we were playing a type of tennis with a football in the gym as we had no classes scheduled for the afternoon. I was summoned by my boss from his office to go to the squadron Admin office. I tracked up to the building thinking to myself "What have I done now?". In the Admin office I was given a small 3" x 2" white box. "Sign here," said the clerk. "It's your GSM," he said. I opened the box and there was a shiny silver General Service Medal (GSM) with a bar saying South Arabia. Again over seven years late. Isn't admin a wonderous thing? I asked about Cyprus, thinking I was on a roll as it was deemed an emergency when I was sent out there. Records said there was no medal struck for the time I was there. Makes me wonder why I took my personal weapon with me. That being the SMG.

Garry was born and we were a family. We had our ups and downs like any others. Jennifer had her nights out as did I, but we seemed to maintain the family way of life without trauma. Now onto our first meeting with Mum.

Mum had previously met Jennifer when I brought her home to introduce her. We travelled in the Worsley Hornet car that I had been buying from Mum. Yorkshire to Essex. Mum hated Jennifer instantly. The end came during our visit when I took Jen up a cup of tea the first morning of our stay. Mother commented I had never ever done that for her. Perversely, up until I was around 12, I was summoned to the bathroom when Mum was having a bath so I could wash her back with a flannel. She would try to cover her breasts without much success, and I hated doing this chore. Tea! What was she thinking to chastise me over such a trivial thing? We are going, I said, as things had become heated. Not in that car, she said. It's not yours. I submitted that I had paid £135 towards its purchase and put in improvements such as a new dashboard and radio. Mother ran upstairs and came down with the cash. Jen and I walked to the bus stop, we were going to stay in London overnight and get the train back later the following day. Prior to our train journey back, we strolled down Oxford Street and went into a well-known jewellery shop. I bought Jen a beautiful ring in the style of the late Princess Diana's ring. Quite an expensive purchase for me in early 1968: £40.00. Jen wore it until we got back, and she wanted to break it to her parents gently. The pregnancy ruled that out of course.

I knew I had damaged my left leg badly as I flew into the tackle, trying to pull the opponent over my left leg as his forwards hit me going the other way. I was playing rugby sometimes three times a week, sometimes for other regiments who seemed to have a famine of Full Backs throughout the garrison. I was taken to hospital. Within a day or two I had a lateral meniscectomy. The surgeon explained they also had to do an investigative procedure to make sure my kneecap was ok because when they opened the knee all the bits of cartilage fell out. Ten days and the stiches were coming out. Jennifer visited dressed up to the nines and obviously going out on the town or worse. Nothing I could do about it. So, like all the other married men on the ward we were allowed to have a bath with our wives in attendance. All the guys in the ward smiled as we walked down the ward to the bathroom to have a bath and whatever occurred to us being alone. I'll leave this to your imagination.

The doc said as I was a PTI I had to go to Chessington which was a Rehabilitation Centre. On arrival at the rehabilitation Centre, I was sent up the hill about a quarter of a mile from the dining area and the gyms. Then back up to sleep in the evenings and so on. This arrangement meant a bit of walking each day and

I always remember one poor guy who it took almost half an hour to do the walk. So, breakfast, dinner and tea meant he was doing his exercise before his exercises. Of course, eventually it occurred to me that this was deliberately done. The aforementioned guy had slept under a tank on exercise to keep out of the rain and the tank of course gradually sank. Luckily, he was saved before being completely crushed, but had sustained a crushed pelvis and leg injuries.

In the gym for the first time (early legs) I was warned by other inmates, don't stand up or get off your mat. I was prepared. There was a gym bench for the instructor to sit on and we faced him as if we were in a theatre and he was onstage. It turns out that if you broke any rules, it was ten press-ups. In came the PTI from the Army Physical Training Corps. All instructors were Physiotherapist trained. To my delight on came some light rock music. He sat down facing us and appeared to be doing nothing. Pointing a finger at me he said TEN. What? As I was doing the ten push ups the guy sitting next to me said, you must do exactly what he's doing. Look at his thumb! There it was on his left hand going backwards and forwards like the pendulum of a clock. I caught on and next two thumbs then an arm. After all the sit-down exercises including the only leg one, I remember, leaning forwards (both hands either side of your knee, you had to raise your stiff leg) the music ended, and we were allowed to stand and enter the main gym. Inside before we did any exercises on the machines, we had an assessment by a doctor. We started to rotate around the various machines until the session was over. The evenings were not without incident. Of course, I was involved.

I was at the bar chatting with a slightly shorter guy than me, but he had a barrelled chest and quite muscular arms. I was of course a full Corporal, and he was also in the Signals. The Signalman and I were chatting, he told me he was from Scotland which was obvious due to his accent. In came a L/Cpl in the Military Police. We had heard about him as he was bragging, mostly to the women, of his ability to handle himself as he had been specially trained. We had also heard some of the other men housed in his spider block had thrown some of his kit out of a window as they were fed up with him. What transpired between Jock and him I do not know but suddenly Jock was facing him, and the Cop was saying he would knock his block off. Oh man! Said Jock, I would F....g kill you. There was a small conservatory leading off the bar. I should have stopped it there and then as the senior rank, but I had full confidence in Jock and this young pratt needed taking down a peg or two. I stood just outside as they squared up to each other. The cop had his palms open as if to be able to chop like a Karate master. Jock had his shoulders rounded and clenched fists and looked the business. A lateral karate swipe about chest high completely missing everything except fresh air and Jock was on him like a puma. Fists were landing. I moved in as Jock was kneeling on him and just making a mess of the super cop's face. It took all my strength to get Jock off his opponent and I dragged him back into the bar. He was shaking with fury. Crashing into the bar came the drenched and bloody cop. At this stage I ordered him out. The girls in the bar were screaming and the blood-soaked cop was shouting as he was led away to the medical centre by possibly the only friend that this idiot had. Jock and I had another beer and headed up to bed a quarter of a mile away.

I was summoned to the CO's office the next day to explain why as the senior Cpl in the bar I had not stopped the fight.

First, I outlined the behaviour of the cop. The reluctance of my bar friend Jock to initially fight the idiot. In my opinion it was two men at odds with each other and I seem to remember the cop saying nothing would happen to Jock as he was about to strike a senior ranked man. As a final explanation I mentioned it was me that pulled off Jock to stop the fight ending in real harm to the plod. It seems with the history of the cop and my explanation resulted in no more action being taken.

A week had passed, and after a quick run around the inside of the gym it was deemed by the doctor that I could be upgraded into "Leg Inters". The same routine except we were introduced to a RAF woman whose name evades me, maybe it was Sally. She was brilliant. Another week and I was in "Lates". Our WRAF nurse/physio took us out bike riding around Chessington area. This time although we were now cross country running, I had to wait another week before going into the advanced group and the chance of going home the following week. Finally, the day came when I headed home.

At last, my First-Class trade course B1. Cable Jointing with Mac up at Winney Hill where I was many years later to become Deputy Line Group Supervisor. Now fully qualified for Sergeant. Ha! Ha!

No real news about us as we dealt with the baby. What next? We had to get a car – £648 bought me a brand-new Triumph Herald 1360 Estate on the "Never, never". I travelled down to the Leyland car factory to pick it up. As usual things were not easy. On inspection the flap behind the rear seats would not sit flat when you wanted to lower the seats to form a bigger carrying area. They spent three hours trying to fix it. In the end I accepted the car in a not-perfect condition as it was going to be midnight before I got home. Once again having driven at 30 miles an hour as per running in of the new car according to the manual, I parked it outside our little end terraced house that we had been given a couple of months previously. Quite handy, opposite the chip shop on Shute Road. There was a babysitter who went off home and I waited for Jen to arrive from her latest night out. Next day we drove around as if we were in a Rolls-Royce.

December 1971. Time to move again. This time we were off to Germany. Bunde, it was the pits; I did argue with the postings officer who offered me 4 Div instead. I should have taken that. Anyway, there was a problem as there were no available married quarters. Jen's dad refused to take Jen and Garry in until I could find married quarters eventually, I think Pam took them in at a price.

I took the ferry over to Zeebrugge and drove down southwards towards Bunde. I parked up in the town not knowing where the barracks were. I saw what looked like two soldiers walking along the pavement. I ran up to them saying do you know where 2 Div barracks are? OOPS, SOXMIS (Soviet Military Mission). The two men were of course Russian. They shook their shoulders but of course they could speak perfect English and would have known where our camp was. The Russian delegation were on occasions invited into our camp or to attend a firing demonstration on a chosen range. All part of the "Look at what we have got so don't mess with us".

They wandered off and I went into the nearest bar. "Bitte" is German for Please. I was about to try my German on the barman. Ein beer bitte please. What a dick I thought. He looked and poured the pint of lager. I had just asked for a beer and said, "Please" in German followed by Please in English. Of course, a garrison town would be quite fluent in English and the barman directed me to the camp.

Once again, I was to become a mortal enemy of my new Squadron OC. Major Sampson. He was, in my opinion, as useful as a one-legged man in an arse kicking contest. Many years later (this is only rumour) he was discharged following an affair with someone's wife in Ireland.

I was now a First-Class tradesman and had my First-Class Education Certificate eligible for Sergeant. Well not in this lifetime, according to Sampson. As a line corporal it was my responsibility to run the cables between vehicles on exercise. Here is a little explanation as to the set-up. My apologies to anyone who disagrees but I am getting very old as I type the explanation. There were two units in our area that provided Comms in a wartime environment. MAIN and STEP UP. Identical and as one ran the Comms, the other would move and hide. At some point the Hiding Unit opened Comms as the Main unit closed. As can be seen, that meant the enemy would have a hard time finding the unit as we toggled between the two units and in different places.

Later I was sent to a set-up called REAR. More about that later.

The only thing Sampson helped with, was finding a married quarter for us. The flat was in a town/area called Lubbecke; the distance to camp in Bunde was about ten miles.

Our trade was about to get an upgrade. A new trade called a TELE-MECH was being formed. I asked for an interview and Major Sampson said, quote: "There are more deserving men in the troop than you!" Application to attend the course refused! I was fuming. He didn't respond or maybe he didn't hear me when as I walked out, I said, "You can fuck off". Looking back some would say a Corporal should not be telling a Major to go away with jerky movements.

This was a trade I could eat!! I needed a strategy to beat this lump of lard commonly known as the OC. Now I needed to be devious. If I can sort a safe out, I could beat this brick wall. In a second as I walked out of his office, I knew what to do. I went straight to the Admin Officer of the Regiment who just so happened to captain the rugby team. Sampson was furious when my course allocation was confirmed. I know this because I was on duty one night as Orderly Corporal and you had to sleep on a bunk bed in the offices. I wandered around, bored, and then noticed the filing cabinet in the troop office was unlocked. I rummaged through the files and found my file. In the folder was a note from my beloved OC. Ref my course. "I specifically said he was not to get this course." I don't know how but he has got away with it again!

Prior to my course we had an exercise, and my crew, me, and Eddie my signalman was the last detachment at our final location. We collected all the cables only to find the whole of Step up parked in a layby a few miles out of town. This group was supposed to be doing the comms NOW!! Main should have shut down. The Corporal in charge of the convoy packet waved us down. "What has happened?" I said. We were waiting for Staff Sergeant ****** who was to take us to the next location, but he never turned up.

I was to go onto the next location as per my orders, the location after the location these guys were supposed to be at. Conscious that someone should know where this lot were, I decided to take them to my next location so someone could sort this mess out. We arrived and found the unit had moved. and was functioning at my location. Major Sampson went berserk! I don't know what happened to Staff Sergeant****** but it wouldn't have been pleasant promotion-wise.

I moved on to Rear, another blot somewhere in the woods. When we arrived all the guys had a good laugh and they said there was a new Major in charge of Rear. Nothing to report until the next evening as we were told the Rodneys (Officers on the exercise) had decided to a have a field Officers Mess dinner. Mess kit and all…Red coats etc. Well as we were sat around the fire at our location waiting to see if any of the Senior ranks had the balls to bring some beer with them because it was supposed to be a DRY exercise, an imposing figure arrived. "I can't believe these people," the figure said. He sat down and said, "Where's the beer?" You knew as soon as he sat down this man was the real deal. Major ****** was our new Rear officer. Ex SAS. That says it all.

In order of events. I had volunteered at about the age of 20 to join 216 para signals. So off to Pre-Parachute training in Aldershot. Of course, I was now 26 and working on a pot belly. I won't go into the poor attempt at pre-para in Aldershot. After a few weeks my left leg was not standing up to the long runs and heavy-duty physical training anymore. Of course, I had undergone a meniscectomy or two on that leg, and after all I had retired (I thought). My left shin burnt each time I tried to keep up with the other three men on my course. Doc agreed and I was sent back to Germany. The smirk on Sampson's face was unbearable but in fairness justified, had I have been given the chance at 20 to do the course when I first applied, I would have been wearing wings in less than two months. Some years later I did do a freefall course – maybe I will remember that later as it was a little exciting.

Back home after the exercise and marking time for my course. My trade re-configuration from Lineman into Telecommunications Mechanic was about to happen. I left the family and headed back to Catterick. Looking back, I believe the course was six weeks long and apart from the 8 Signals boring admin issues such as making the course leader by default in alphabet ranking, and there were no men on my course with a surname beginning with "A", you can guess who became course leader.

Whinny Hill was still there as I remember from my basic training. Mr MacSkimming, the Scotsman who was the civilian Cable Jointing Instructor, was there, smiling as he greeted us all on day one in the jointing room. How are you doing, Brownie? He said with a smile. Hello, Mac, I said. I felt at home. I strolled through the course, pretty much top again.

Nobody knew my new trade disciplines. Back in Germany I think I was the first Tele Mech in Germany. Nobody in the Line or Tech world knew how to treat me. What was this new trade called Telecommunications Mechanic? Where do we put him? Sampson was practically frothing during my post-course return, especially as my report was glowing and my excellent report from Catterick, I feel sure it made him nauseous. The interview with Major Sampson on my return went as I expected. Having read my course report, Major Sampson said, "You seem to have pulled your socks up". I knew there was no such slots in my regiment for my new trade. I stood there at attention. Couldn't keep my mouth shut could I. "There never was anything wrong with my socks, sir!" "Don't be insolent with me, Corporal," he yelled. I could hear all the other staff in the corridor sniggering. They probably said to themselves Oh! It's Brown again. My last words to Major S: "Sir, would this be an inopportune time for a posting?" He shouted back, "I will recommend it." Yeah! A result.

I think I had been to heading home from the Buffalo Lodge called "The Mailed Fist". I admit I had had a few and reached the top of the woodland ridge, which was a T-junction. It was midnight and I always look for oncoming lights. Anyway, I braked to about five miles an hour and turned left. After about ten seconds I saw car lights in my rear-view mirror. I put my foot down as I knew that in about ten minutes, I would be home. The lights kept coming at a fast rate. What made me slow was the blue flashing light. I wound down the window, taking heavy breaths, hoping the cops would not smell my breath. Typical German Police, one of the cops approached me after getting out of the open topped Porsche. He didn't look at me, just stood close enough for me see his gun. He spewed out a lot of German which he must have known I probably didn't speak as my car had BFG plates. After he stopped, I said, "I am sorry, I don't speak German." He said I had not stopped at the T junction. That was a 20 Mark fine. Luckily in Germany you can pay the fine to the cop. This I did, he took the money, I got a receipt. I was on my way. Phew!!

Jen and I had two girls in Germany, both of whom were made British Citizens after a visit to the consulate. Tracey, the youngest, was a tomboy and when eligible for Infants school always wore jeans underneath her dress. She hasn't changed much in all those years, except she doesn't go to Infants school anymore.

In case I forget, a little about my children. Garry was born in Catterick, North Yorkshire. Because Jen and I were always in another country, Garry spent some time in boarding school. The school was Scorton Grammar in North Yorkshire and later in the Lees in Hoy Lake, Liverpool. Nothing really outstanding with Garry, those moments came later in life.

From what I remember about four weeks after Jen gave birth to Karen, our oldest daughter, we had a visitor. The visitor was a Lt Col whose first name was Jeff. Apparently, Jeff was the Chief Chaplain, I believe in BAOR but again, memory is having a devastating effect on my recollections. Jeff was doing the washing up as I came home one late afternoon. Jeff introduced himself. It seems as I put fingers to typing keys that I have always been associated with drunks. Jeff really liked his whisky, come to that almost any alcoholic beverage. One evening George Drysbrough, a signalman in my unit, and his wife had also just welcomed a newborn to swell the British population in Germany. George and his wife came over for (you guessed it) drinks one evening, when there was a knock on the door. Hello, Jeff, I said. Jeff sat down and was suitably refreshed when the subject of christening came up. I think at that time there was snow on the ground, and I maintained it would be too cold to take a baby out in this weather to get to the church. No problem, said Jeff. Practicalities sprung into my mind. "But, Jeff," I said, "what about a font etc for the holy water etc?" Again, no problem, said Jeff. We can use a saucepan with tap water. Don't worry, I will bless the water; thereon it was to be holy water. WHAT! Both children were christened in the little flat. The holy water and the fragrance of whisky and Heineken completed the solemn ceremony. About a year later

Tracy was born in the same hospital as Karen. Three kids in two years, whew! I would fix this issue later in Holland.

A brief interlude. Kids' schooling. Marsden Hall where my girls were to be educated was run by ex-signals Major Gardiner and his wife in Bridlington. I am not sure about their academic qualifications, but the school was well staffed, and all the children seemed very happy.

The Major's wife always seemed buoyant and happy. One Christmas school holiday I took the old Triumph to get the girls, bringing them back to Darlington where we had bought our first house, a modern end-terraced house. Little story coming later about it. I entered the stairway in Marton Hall and the Major's wife came running down the stairs and said the girls would be ready in about 15 minutes. "Would you like to go downstairs for a drink?" she said. In the huge cellar underneath Marton Hall was a bar! About half a dozen of the staff were in various stages of merriment. After I had a couple of pints, the girls were deemed ready to leave by the Major's wife who decided to stop at the bar. Later when I was trying to keep tabs on my finances, I noticed that Marton Hall's cheque had not been cashed. On investigation there was apologies from the school, and I quote "The cheque was found behind the piano". Enough said.

I am informed today the Major Gardiner is deceased and possibly his alcoholic wife.

Back to our house in Darlington. Tracey loves animals. We got her a rabbit which I housed in our garden shed. I so regret all that happened with the rabbit. Unknown to me, I put newspaper in the hutch. Should have been straw. The rabbit developed growth around its mouth and one morning was found dead. I consoled Tracey and we wrapped the body in a bin bag. The garden was a bit triangular and at its point divided by a wooden division which joined a public footway into a school playing field. I decided to bury the rabbit in the tiny triangular plot. Years later I went back to see my old house. I parked facing the front door and a woman came out. I explained I had once lived in her house. The lady invited me in and showed me all the alterations they had made. As her husband and I drank tea, I mentioned the rabbit. Oh yes!! she spoke. Initially when the body was first found it was thought to be a baby skeleton. A murder investigation ensued. Of course, it was soon discontinued after forensics deemed it to be a rabbit carcass.

A small car crash in Bielefeld underground car park where I was coming from the right and a car smashed into my little Triumph. The businessman eventually paid for the repair after several weeks of delay. I only mention this crash as later my newly repaired car was again damaged, on my return to Germany, gratis ice, and a level crossing just over a small bridge.

Soon after I was off to AFCENT. Allied Forces Central Europe. Headquarters in Brunssum in the Netherlands. Currently, I believe, it is called Allied Joint Force Command. I was sent to 227 Signal Squadron not far from Maastricht.

We were to live in the British Forces Accommodation in a place called HEER. My working life was done on exercises or in Tapijn Kazern, Maastricht, our little 227 Sigs stronghold.

I knew a couple of the lads and I was made welcome for a change and my Foreman of Signals, Terry, along with another Foreman, Brian, was pleasant enough until Brian who was Jewish had a falling out in my new Buffalo Lodge. One of the fines in a Buffalo Lodge is for not paying your dues. Stupidly, I brought Brian up on a charge for not paying his Jews. I know, childish, but at that time I thought it was funny. Brian, not so much.

Our next-door neighbour was a Chief Tech in the Royal Airforce. Jen was very active in the wife's nights out scene. Parties were frequent and Ray our neighbour and his wife may have been swappers, but I hadn't noticed it at the time. I did notice Ray and Jen did a lot of dancing together and there was so much going on with the married wives and single men. I won't dwell on that. After a while we got into some form of routine. Sundays was me preparing the Sunday Dinner. All Jen had to do was cook it after I returned from Louis's Bar at 3.00 pm. All of us from the troop housed in Heer who liked a Sunday drink went to Louis's Bar. What I liked about Louis was we never paid until the end. If you bought a round, he would mark on your own beer mat how many beers you had purchased and you paid at the end.

We had a silly game called "Fingers". The best description I can give is, the first man to start in a clockwise direction would say a number, let's say 12. Because he is starting, he would say 12, clicking his left finger/thumb (like the Spanish castanets) each time and repeating with his right hand calling the same number. Next, he would do this again but the second number he called could be the same number so the person on his left could not make a call unless the number had changed. Now everyone after the initial two-handed opening would raise their hands in the air shouting FINGERS, wiggling the fingers and smack both hands down on the table and the next person in rotation would repeat the last of the two fingers using the castanets routine. So, we shout FINGERS (arms raised in the air wiggling fingers) hands slapped down on the table palms down, we clapped next, then arms raised, and castanets. Left, right but the first number called must be the last number repeated. Say this is the second sequence. 12, 9, so, wriggling fingers, slap down both hands, clap, raise hands castanets with the last number (9) and your number, let's say 48, with the next. The next player following the routine would call let's say 48, and his number. If a player hesitated or messed up in the routine or got the numbering wrong, he paid a round. WHEW! Perhaps I should have left that bit out. Louis's wife was called Margret who was a large lady like you see on the Beer Festival films. Margret wore a low-cut dress showing what can only be described as ample cleavage. Now I like big chested women, but Margret also sported a couple of grey hairs about two inches long that really quelled any attraction for me.

Nick Besant was a REME Sergeant who lived in the flat above ours. The poor old Triumph needed a new wheel bearing, and it was nearly finished as he came up to me and said with some sympathy, "Your mum's died!"

Jen and I decided that only I should return to the UK for the funeral. The Quarter Master at camp arranged extra petrol coupons if I needed them. Money if I needed it, which I didn't. I set off to drive to Calais, made the ferry and drove to Plymstock in Devon having no incidents along the way.

I drove up to the little bungalow and Dad answered the door. Short on words he said, Hello! We sat in the kitchen and drank a cup of tea. Unknown to me, Mum was lying in the bedroom. "Want to see your Mum?" he said. I was reluctant as I think at that time, she would have been the first dead body I had ever seen. I was truly shocked. She was dressed in what I can only describe as a doll's frilly lace nightgown. She had shrunk from her 5ft 4" frame to a prostrate body of what seemed to me to be about 4ft. The skin on her face was like marble. Dad, to my amazement, went to her and kissed her forehead. Now the weird part. (I do not believe in the supernatural or ghosts of any kind.) I thought that I should follow Dad's example. To this day I swear as I kissed that ice cold forehead, she frowned! I took it that she was regretting how she had treated me and maybe I had forgiven her. I had not! But nobody should die like that. I remember visiting nurses turning her when she had taken herself to bed on a previous short visit, and she screamed. No amount of Valium could offset the pain she was going through. Mum and Dad must have been married over 45 years. Why? I thought, especially during their fights. An attempted stabbing by her into the back of Dad or the event in the garden where Dad charged at her with the clothes prop shouting "You cancerous cow!" – at that time, I don't think she had been diagnosed with cancer. Sad but it must have been true they loved each other at some time.

I knew she had had cancer years in the past. Mum and Dad only entertained (which was practically never) in the front room, otherwise it was in the kitchen. About five years had passed since her diagnosis. Much to her disgust, I had married Jen and we took Garry to see her and Dad for the first time. Garry was just about crawling. We were in the kitchen and Mum sat there with pursed lips as I cleaned up Garry's face after he brought up some recently drunk milk from his bottle. The tension was awful. I decided to get Garry's nappy off and clean him up on the kitchen floor. I have no idea how Jen felt or even what she was doing as I was trying to minimize the time my mother was watching Garry. I thought, put Garry in the front room, let him crawl around and we could thrash out any of Mum's gripes. I think that was the last time Jen ever saw her. I don't even remember what the outcome was. What I do remember is that when any discussion was over, I went into the pristine front room to get Garry and there he was crawling around happily, and I thought never mind, we are going home from this hell hole. Just one thing to do. Pick up the very large poop Garry had done on Mum's holy carpet!

Me and Dad, Aunt Fay, Sandra, and Uncle Ed attended the short ceremony at the crematorium. I watched the coffin being engulfed in flames before the doors shut. No real emotion I don't think, but on exit, as we said goodbye to the vicar I started to cry. Aunt Fay turned and said, "It seems so final." As a non-believer, I can tell you it is! Another thing she said was "Life passes so quickly". Yep! so I had better get on with this, time is passing very quickly.

Time to lighten the mood and prepare my memory for my next attempt at writing and my many years living in Maine, USA.

A Joke, American style

After their 11th child, a Kentucky couple decided that was enough as they could not afford any more kids. So, the husband went to his doctor and told him that he and his wife didn't want to have any more children. The doctor told him that there was a procedure called a vasectomy that could fix the problem but that it was expensive. "A less costly alternative," said the doctor, "is to go home, get a cherry bomb (fireworks are legal in Kentucky), light it, put it in a beer can, then hold the can up to your ear and count to 10. The Kentuckian said to the doctor, "I may not be the smartest tool in the shed, but I don't see how putting a cherry bomb in a beer can next to my ear is going to help me."

"Trust me," said the doctor. So, the man went home, lit a cherry bomb, and put it in a beer can. He held the can up to his ear and began to count! "1, 2, 3, 4,5", at which point he paused, placed the beer can between his legs and continued counting on his other hand. This procedure also works in Tennessee, Louisiana, Mississippi, parts of Georgia, Missouri, West Virginia, and all of Washington DC.

Back to AFCENT. I played rugby for AFCENT but, we were not a very good team. Too many nationalities wanting to show their abilities and of course they didn't have many of those and I was slowing up too.

I was on exercise travelling back to base. With all the heavy cables (Quad,14pr etc) the Governed 3 tonner would only travel at just over 30 miles per hour. I was sick of it. Exercise over, I chatted to my REME mate and asked if he could take the governor out so the 3 tonners could travel at a reasonable speed.

Cruising down the autobahn with just the Foreman and senior sergeants in the back of a Land Rover waving at me and my passenger, I felt the urge to be aggressive. I waved them on and flashed them as the 3 tonner was like a Lamborghini. Everyone was laughing as we topped around 60mph. It then happened! A large bang! At that time, I didn't know the full extent of the problem until I saw in the wing mirror lumps of metal flying all over the autobahn. Brakes had gone! Metal flying everywhere. I used the handbrake and eventually we stopped. I ran back as there was debris all over the motorway and cars were swerving to dodge the wreckage spin offs. On went the four-way flashers from our vehicles. I threw what bits I could, such as the part of the broken prop shaft, into the back of the vehicle. The

Land Rover crew called out the REME Wreckage Crew and the dead 3 tonner was towed back to camp.

Several days later I was presented with the 18-inch remnant of the prop shaft all newly painted in black with a white inscription saying, "Keith's and the date". Just checking my Little Red Book which says I was there from December 1972 until June 1975.

I seem to have done well in Holland and was sent back to England for two years as a Sergeant with the Army Youth Team stationed in Litchfield, Staffordshire.

Before taking up the team Sergeant position, I was sent on a Unit Expedition Leaders course in Towyn, Wales.

I had bought a new pair of walking boots which I had never really used for any distance walking. Day one on the course after a day of trekking around the knife edge of Snowdon, we continued to Beddgelert and up Moel Hebog in Gwynedd. My feet were killing me, and I had cavernous holes in my heels. That night my Royal Navy buddy who shared a tent with me decided to become a medic and had this cream which apparently would help when applied to my heels. He applied the cream, I nearly screamed as I clenched my teeth, ears ringing. The tent flap opened and in came the instructor for the course. Looking at my heels he took us all back to camp the following day. On arrival the medical staff applied a sticky sponge padded dressing with large holes cut out so the wounds could breathe and boots from the camp clothing store were issued.

Next day we were off again, and I reminisced about my basic climbing course years in the past. Just to let you know what crazy military personalities we have in our wonderful military. My instructor, Pete B, at that time had an Alsatian. He had made a backpack for the dog, explaining the dog carried its own food etc. When we came to climbing (only happened once) he picked up the dog and laid it across his shoulders and started to climb. The dog was not too impressed and whimpered until on Terra Ferma once again.

Final day of the course and we were to meet the transport back to camp. Walking alongside the river I recalled much of my climbing books such as Eric Langmuir whose information included "River Crossings" were recalled. Again, I could not hold back and luckily for me being the senior man on the course didn't care what hardship to my fellow course members who in my eyes would not have completed a course like this without doing a river crossing. (Looking back at my recollections it is no wonder that I have not been liked by everyone I have met!) So, after an uneventful crossing using several techniques, we boarded the bus back to camp and the final completion of the course.

As team Sergeant with 67 Army youth team, based in Whittington Barracks not far from Litchfield, I taught Map Reading and Canoeing with other duties such as The Duke of Edinburgh's Award Scheme. As team Sergeant I went with my team to schools mainly in Newcastle under Lyme area to promote the Army and recruiting those interested in joining after they had left school. Orienteering was also a favourite, especially during the expedition aspect for the Awards we supported. On part of the course the runners had to find what was written on a gravestone in a small cemetery. I am not really into poetry but the one poem I remember to this day was when doing an orienteering recce. The inscription on the gravestone went like this.

Remember men as you pass by
As you are now, so once was I
As I am now you will surely be
Be prepared to follow me.

As we all know I am not religious but if I were it might be worth thinking about.

The good thing about the team was that we never worked in the mornings. Afternoons were spent on useless projects like building our own fibre glass canoes (none ever turned out right and so that project was abandoned quite early during our futile attempts to save money). Climbing in Wales was popular especially in Llanberis. We visited schools, usually in Newcastle under Lyme, helping children to gain their Duke of Edinburgh's Award Scheme qualifications.

The day arrived when Frank, our Youth Team boss, was posted, and we had our new boss, he was a warrant officer with no experience in anything outdoors. Just a short note here as his name escapes me. I was taking a bunch of children climbing – just easy stuff – when my new boss turned up with his girlfriend. Obviously, they were well prepared as she was wearing high heels, and he sported a motorcycle helmet. God help us!! I made my thoughts clear, and it wasn't too long before they left. Not much more to tell about the team.

Jen and the family had now settled into our new quarter in Whittington Barracks. Jen had found a job in Birmingham and commuted daily. I played a lot of golf and managed to get a 22 handicap.

The kids were in a local school, and all seemed to have calmed down, except one afternoon Jen turned up with a

Warrant Officer, I think from the Gloucestershire Regiment. Weird, I don't remember the outcome of that meeting, but by this time I was seeking other company.

Just setting off to go to our office, my hand on the knocker having closed the door, I froze. A van with TV Licensing displayed drove up to the house. A man shouted to me: "Are they in?" No, I shouted back. They drove off and I drove to the Post Office to get a TV Licence.

Another night out for Jen. An office party in Birmingham. She wanted me to pick her up at the railway station at midnight. The station was opposite the bus station on the opposite side of the road. The bus station had straight through run-in run-out system. However, there was a very high privet alongside the exit so no view of the traffic coming out of the bus station exit for the normal traffic in the opposite direction.

I had four pints of beer out of the fridge and watched the TV and finally took off to pick up Jen.

Midnight and I waited outside the front of the railway station. No Jen! So, I drove across the road to the bus station in case she had got a bus back instead. No Jen! One last look at the railway station and I pulled out of the bus station, blinded by the privet. An oncoming taxi and I hit head on. Luckily it was a 30-mile limit on that road. Unfortunately, the taxi went on to hit a telegraph pole; however, the driver was not hurt. My front dashboard was pushed back and trapped my left thigh briefly. The police were on the scene very quickly as they were in the multi-storey car park and heard the noise of the collision. I awaited my fate, having blown into the breathalyser. The cop holding the recording device showed it to his partner and said,

Clear! What! So, no drink and drive. My car was towed off and the cops drove me home.

When I arrived home Jen was there. What the F. I was fuming as she said she had sent a message to the guard room to say she was getting a lift home and not to worry. I went into a sulk and went to bed with a badly bruised raw left femur. The car was gone and, luckily, I drove the Troop's Land Rover for the rest of the time until we were next posted. Two years had nearly passed, just another course to get into by way of a change, before our next posting.

Parachuting was still in my blood, and I so wanted to experience jumping out of a plane. I applied for the course and was successful. I arrived at the jump school and was teamed up with some 216 para guys. Although they were very experienced jumpers, they had never done Freefall. One recognised me and I was accepted into their fold.

Day one revolved around parachute packing and we were told these were the ones we were to jump with in two days' time. (Don't panic, Mr M.) Other activities were running backwards and forwards to a drop zone target, hanging onto suspended parachute harnesses practising hang ups and twisted lines etc, and my favourite, jumping off a 4ft gymnasium box.

As an experienced Physical Training Instructor, I noticed straight away a tall man who was apparently in the Guards and his landing off the box. Most of us raised our arms as if holding the parachute lines/toggles, landing with feet together. On impact with the ground with legs together rolling onto one's side. Correct method! The guardsman was landing straight legged, and I was surprised that the Staff Instructors didn't pick up on it.

The old twin engine Rapide aircraft revved up on the grass runway. Of course, not only the senior ranked trainee on the course and of course the alphabetical first on the course as there was, as usual, nobody on the course with a name beginning with an "A", I was to be "number one out".

Although excited I think most of us eight jumpers were nervous as the old aircraft trundled over the grassland and eventually rose into the air over a place call NEW Zealand Farm.

Sgt Major Lang, the jump master, was looking nervous and looking at his altimeter. We were to jump at 2600 feet. Suddenly, he said OUT! I said it's not 2600, he said look. I looked out of the open fuselage door and saw flames coming out of the engine. Unknown to me at that time the engine block had cracked and the flames I saw were those each time the engine pistons fired. "It's alright for you," Lang said. "I must stay with the aircraft."

Onto the wing, off at the tap on my side and shouting as instructed, thousand and one, thousand and two etc, but I lost all procedure thoughts as I had my strings around my throat. Training says kick your legs to spin the chute. I just got hold of the strings and pulled them apart as If I was taking off a coat or jacket. The parachute rotated. I was in heaven looking at the scenery and taking no notice of the foghorn from the ground staff. A bit late I did control the parachute but by this time I was preparing to land in a ploughed farmer field narrowly missing a barbed wire fence. However, I was only about 150 yards from the drop zone. I picked up my chute and raced back to repack for another jump. An Islander plane had been brought in for the rest of the jumps that day but as we were watching the rest of the course landing from the ground and we were busy packing our chutes, suddenly there was panic as the instructors raced off in a Land Rover across the fields.

Shortly after, the Islander took off. The ground to air radio was blaring through the speakers close to us at ground zero. "Screaming" bellowed from the speaker. The pilot said hello, Cambridge. (This was Cambridge hospital, I think a military hospital at the time.) Arrival five minutes. The patient seems to be in some pain. Apparently, the guardsman had landed obviously with straight legs and inflicted and received an open fracture of the femur for his efforts.

For the next few days, we practised indoors due to bad weather but on the runway for our second jump a guy from the back of our eight men jump group lost it on the runway just before take-off. He shouted, "I don't want to go." The pilot waited as he was off loaded, and we could see him on the grass looking like a lonely child wanting his mum. Everyone was thinking about the guardsman.

I stood on the wing of the Islander awaiting the tap in my side. As I went into stable position my hand hit the fuselage, but no harm done but a critique later said I had not completed my count.

Third time I gained an excellent review. Fourth jump having spent a day or so practising dummy pulls I rolled on exit, fumbling for the ripcord and was told I would be off the course if I did that again. Obviously if the chute had been deployed, I would have fallen into it. Right call by training staff.

Course was ending as the weather had been so bad and I think only one (a woman in the Military Police) had made freefall. Well done, her! On the bright side I had experienced parachuting.

My two years at the Army Youth team was coming to an end and my posting came through.

Cyprus beckoned again and I wondered at what changes to the island had been made since the dividing of the island between Greece and the Turkish populations. It was now 1978.

Christmas time in the sun but once again lack of posting administration had not included my family.

Having been greeted by a friend or two from previous encounters everyone asked me where my family was. On explanation, within a week my family arrived, and we lived in a lovely bungalow in RAF Akrotiri.

Having a car was essential in Cyprus and friends took me down to see "Charlie A". Charlie had a bit of a scam going on because if he sold a new car he would have had to pay import duty, but if you covered the low price of the car he would buy it back when your tour was over, hence it was a used car. Well, that is how I understood it. I bought a Toyota Corolla.

Kids had a great time there, especially Buttons bay and Ayia Napa.

One day when on leave we decided to find Ayia Napa and pitch tents on the beach. Jen insisted we took the bloody cat. At that time there was only one big hotel alongside the beach, but it was nearing 8.00pm and I saw a small wooden building on the beach and decided to head for it. Naturally we got bogged down in the sand. I walked toward the hut where several volunteers helped me onto firmer ground, and we parked right next to the hut. A Keo beer in hand, having pitched the tents, I thought of breakfast, Halloumi (fried cheese) and eggs and of course a beer. The cat escaped and meowed throughout the night. By this time, I didn't care, and we captured it in the morning.

The lady who ran the hut bar with her Cypriot boyfriend was called Anna and she was English. In the daytime she had a show on British Forces Radio.

As the weeks wore on, we travelled around the Island. I took the family up Troodos Mountain. It was what was classed as winter in Cyprus. Now I was beginning to get some sensibility into my life and prepared by taking snow chains in the boot of the Toyota. I seemed to be at the head of a tiny convoy as we headed up the mountain. The Toyota wheels began to skid, and it was snowing. When I stopped everyone else stopped and of course were unable to continue. I jumped out, got the chains, put them on the rear wheels and off we drove. I thought it was prudent not to wave to my other convoy members. Looking out of the cafe windows towards the sea, sipping a beer, having eaten an excellent trout, I was content.

Later in the year I had been visiting a buffalo lodge up Troodos and coming down passing through a small village a young kid threw what I thought was a small stone at my car window screen. No damage but of course I slammed on the brakes wanting to get hold of this little brat. I skidded and the car swivelled and careered up the first two flight of steps of a shop, damaging the right wing. Instantly there were dozens of locals surrounding the car. My mate was terrified, but I was fuming so I got out of the car. A spokesman for the crowd said the kid had admitted he threw a grape at my windscreen and was sorry. I had calmed down and conscious that this village was pro-EOKA during my previous tour in 1964. Better get moving then. Later in the week I took the car to "Charlie's", and he repaired the damage, saying he would take 50 off my refund when my tour was over. I was happy.

We as a family had a night out at a concert by Patrick Moore in Kourion. Now I think Patrick used to present "Stars at Night" on the UK television many years ago, but of all things he was playing the xylophone and chatting about his life.

Other places we loved to visit were a jetty café that did wonderful battered squid and chips. Paphos was another place we used to frequently go to, and the café used to have two pelicans; however, one died and the second nearly followed by biting me as we sat at our table – however, it was just like having two small wooden planks simultaneously slapping you either side of your forearm. He probably died of old age.

On the beach at Ayia Napa one afternoon we were having a small barbecue, except two small problems occurred. For some reason, Garry, my son, needed to get into the car boot. Having opened the boot, he took out whatever it was he needed and partially closed it, leaving about an inch of the door open. Just as well because he had also dropped the car keys inside the boot. I slightly bent the boot door as I managed to force the door open. And hoped Charlie would not notice. Just as well – things could have become much worse as the rotary spit for the intended chicken barbecue was also in the boot. But the little rotary device failed to work so I stood there for an hour turning the chicken until I considered it was cooked. At least I got that right. I purchased a beach ball for the kids at a small hut which offered things like bucket and spades and other beach contraptions.

Now don't let go of it in the water!

As Jen lay in the sun and the kids had managed to let go of the brand new beachball, I sauntered into the water, having displayed some irritation with the kids after my precise instructions regarding the ball had been ignored. The ball was about twenty feet in front of me. I started a slow breaststroke after the errant ball. Fifteen minutes had passed by, and the ball was twenty feet away. I noted I was quite a way from shore and tried crawl which had no effect on me closing the distance. The waves were getting rather high, and I started to take in a bit of water, and I was near to panic. Now out to sea. I had managed to grab onto this huge buoy, the type that large ships would moor on. I watched as the ball was taken by the strong tide just (you guessed it) twenty feet away.

I hung onto the buoy for about five minutes just to catch my breath and glanced at the shore. The people were minute and of all things I started to sing the "Jaws" film tune. I set off doing the crawl against the tide. I seemed to be getting more distance underwater and I looked down at the sandy bottom as I got closer to the shore. So much relief when my feet touched the sand, and I could see the family. I wondered what their reaction would be. NONE! I said to Jen, "Weren't you concerned?" No! she said. I knew you would be back. What? I had been away over 45 minutes. That completed our wonderful day at the beach.

Jen made friends in her usual way, joining the Ladies Glades which is the equivalent of our Buffalo Order. I became the Deputy Grand Primo for the province and Overseas Rep. As a member of six lodges my social calendar was somewhat full as I also took on the Buffalo Club bar as steward. Jen and I served behind the bar for most social functions. On Sundays I showed "Road Runner" film shows on my Super 8 projector in the club. It was supposed to be for the kids but as the afternoon wore on and alcohol took its toll, most of us adults were creased up at the film's Road Runner antics.

As a Buffalo Province we decided that kids in the UK that were unable to get any form of holiday because their parents could not afford it might be offered a Holiday of a Lifetime. The offer was made to Grand Lodge and they in turn trawled the provinces to find children in need of a holiday.

We made a series of money earning fetes. One member's wife ran a Mystic Rose tent. Palm reading, and Tarot card readings and all that mumbo jumbo. We had various units offering rides on military vehicles. Archery contests and horse rides and much more.

The results were in, and several children were nominated. We had the cash, and the children arrived, and all was gong well until someone suggested the kids could be interviewed on our local military radio about their holiday. I agreed as this would advertise our order and attract more members. One child said he had just come back from somewhere exotic, and it turned out his father was someone quite high up in the buffalo world. I was furious! There is no limit to "A" holes in this world and I refer to the man not the boy.

Disaster in Akrotiri

I was just leaving my bungalow to go to work. I could see the Airbase about half a mile away. There was a big explosion near Air Traffic control. I jumped into the Corolla and set off for the office which was not far from the runway. A little history first about the good old USA and us. Although the USA had no real personnel on the base, that was not true. One of the hangars housed a U-2 which went on various missions over "you know where. Ask Francis Gary Powers". Unfortunately, the original U-2 pilot was killed in a car crash after a night out with some teachers from the children's school on the camp. The US powers had to send to Allied Forces Southern Europe (AFSOUTH) for a replacement as they had tight flying missions over Turkey and beyond. So, our new sky jockey was taking off and apparently wanted to show off a bit. Now the wings of a U-2 are 105ft. When the plane came into land and had slowed to jogging pace, the waiting yanks on the runway ran parallel to the plane, putting extended wheels underneath the wing tips to stop the aircraft falling over. Basically, the U-2 was a rocket glider. But our new pilot obviously forgot the wingspan. He decided turning and climbing at the same time was showing his skills as a new arrival. One wing hit the tarmac and the aircraft disintegrated, barely missing the Control Tower but an engine fell into the Met Office, killing several locally employed weathermen. The wings or one wing full of fuel fell onto the Communications Centre. Mainly housing women operators. The place was ablaze. One hero of this disaster was an RAF man who on hearing the screams jumped into his Land Rover and drove into the side of the flimsy building. (No brickwork involved in the construction of most buildings on the camp.) This heroic act saved most of the lives within that building and he later received some form of commendation for his bravery. The fire service had the whole thing dowsed in a very short time. Everyone was traumatized and it took many weeks for my crew to get all the communication cables extracted from the old cable duct and we replaced those cables with polythene insulated cables.

Another unsung hero was the person who had planned for something like this to happen. That person had set up an

ALTERNATIVE OPS building so all those comms were then switched over when the disaster happened. Brilliant. Another jockey was sent for, along with another U-2.

I was about to replace a telecom cable that went into the U-2 hangar. This was the only hard-wired method of communication they had for their phones etc. I managed to support the old cable that I was jointing to, from the telecom pillar with an old wooden box. (A pillar is just terminations joining cables on the inside of an asbestos-covered cylinder.)

I was just finishing the joint and the blow lamp was in full blast as I was sealing the joint sleeve and wiping the ends. A figure revealed himself, asking me what I was doing alongside the SECURE aircraft hangar. I explained I was putting in a new cable network and that tomorrow I would have to be given access to the offices inside the hangar to complete the installation. The yank said, I would have to be escorted into the hangar.

Now when you are concentrating using a blow lamp you must be careful not to melt anything other than what you want to. So, the blow lamp was directed away on several occasions as I finished work that day. I got the guys from the troop to take the cable drum full of the remaining cable back to our cable compound. So, the story goes that in one of my concentration modes I had withdrawn the flame of the blowlamp to the side, but unknown to me the flame had ignited a small ember inside the cable drum where the bar resided. At about 5.00 the following morning the Camp Fire Brigade was called to our cable compound to extinguish a cable drum ablaze. Quite a lot of money was written off and I was not the most popular Sergeant on camp.

I approached the U-2 hangar and was escorted into the commanding officer's office where the other end of my cable needed re-terminating, effectively marrying up with the pillar outside. Now two things: 1. I was dissuaded into NOT looking at the aircraft as I was walking to the Commander's office; 2. That the comms in their building were said to be very secure. Ha, Ha.

If they only realised that anyone could listen into any phone calls by lifting the pillar cover off and with a pair of clips tag onto any extension with a comms phone and a pair of clips.

As far as the aircraft is concerned, I had no interest at all.

The week before my birthday I got a babysitter, and Jen and I went to the Steak House not far from the camp. We sat down and the local entertainment was in full flow and as we downed a few drinks having finished our food the real party went up a gear. One of the local entertainments was a guy holding a tambourine-type contraption with shelves inside the outer circumference of this wooden tambourine. On the shelves were little shot glasses of ouzo. Our dancer waved the tambourine around and the centrifugal force kept the glasses from flying out, providing he was doing it fast enough. Well, he had already had a few drinks and suddenly in slowing, the glasses were flying around the room. It was like World War Two. People were ducking as the glasses were smashing on the walls and people were getting drenched. Also of course there is the Greek plate smashing thing! No idea what that is about, but apparently, they use special plates. Of course, I was not aware of that and following their plate smashing dance I got our clean plates and smashed them onto the stone floor. I was quickly advised not to continue, and we went home.

A new bar-restaurant had opened on the main road out of camp. The restaurant was called Silvanna's. The reason I mention this night out with the whole family is because it was my birthday, 28th January. The owner/waiter served us and was absolutely one of the friendliest locals I had ever met. I asked about the name of the restaurant, and he said it was his daughter's name and that she was one year old today. I said that it was also my birthday today. Next minute he brought out a big bottle of wine with his compliments and introduced us to his father whose birthday was also that very day. The old man came out and we all lined up doing a typical Greek dance and for once nothing went untoward. In the following months we went back and were always warmly greeted and given a free bottle of wine.

The years had flown by, and we were about to leave Cyprus.

My new posting came through and I was off back to Blandford and CPA, Communications Project Agency.

There were several specialised groups in the agency, and I was in CP6, which dealt with installations. Much of the time I was involved in making switching equipment between actual overseas deployments.

My least enjoyable job was when I was sent to Belize to do a cable installation. As soon as I arrived, I was shown the job by the Foreman of Signals, and it consisted of quite a few big new cables in the exchange that required jointing. Before I was to start a smaller job, I was to fix a broken phone line that was somewhere in the jungle. The line was suspended from trees and the odd hut. I found a break in the cable and had climbed into a tree to secure the twin cable when I fell. Below me as I fell was what I can only describe as a piece of concrete not unlike a kerbstone. For once I was unhurt and as described earlier in this dribble, I was quite competent at falling over.

A person appeared looking down at me from the hut not ten feet from where I lay. Are you alright? The man said. Yes, thanks, I replied. What are you doing? he said. I explained that I had found the fault in the cable that I was sent by Airfield Troop to repair. Well, don't go near this hut, he said.

And at that time, I was in a shock because yet again I had managed to brush with the SAS. Thinking back, it was a communication hut for their jungle sorties. We were at the height of the Belizean-Guatemalan territorial dispute. I am not going to get into explaining this dispute as it went on for years. I left the area, having fixed the cable, and headed back to camp.

During the evenings, the Sergeants' mess laid on entertainment, but all I was interested in was getting back to Blandford. Even the young women who had left their outer toilet door open and lifted their dresses, exposing their bodies, trying to elicit a joining of bodies for a few pennies had no effect as my mind was set. It was getting close to the end of my jointing job. I had 3,254 pair cables left. I finished all the jointing in one session, and it was gone two o'clock in the morning when I had finished. I went to bed. At close to nine o'clock I was awoken by the Foreman who ranted at me. I explained how I had worked through the night and the installation, and my work done here. I'll tell you when you're finished here, he ranted. He really needed me, but I was not under his employment, and I was about to go into my well-known rebellious mode. As soon as I was able, I was on the phone to Blandford. I explained the situation and as my actual job had been completed, I was on a plane back to the UK within two days. No number of trips to the close islands on our days off were going to keep me here.

Back in Blandford I was told we were going to Nepal. A radio system was to be installed. All the new radio equipment was loaded onto a Hercules aircraft. Off we went via Cyprus and Bahrain. I do remember visiting old friends in Cyprus and again after a drink-filled evening sprinting down to the airport in the morning to grab my stuff and then onto the plane, securing myself with my belt through the cargo netting covering the equipment. Lying on top of the equipment. Best place as the seating was minimal and I just wanted to sleep.

In Bahrain we stayed overnight which was memorable, lounging in an infinity pool after having eaten snails for the first time. We had inflight catering paying for everything, so no constraints on how much free booze we consumed. Refreshed the following day, we boarded the plane again and were to experience seeing the Himalayas. I remember us having to circle as we descended to land in Kathmandu. Now known as Tribhuvan International Airport. Initially billeted in a local hotel but finally in Dharan. The British Gurkha Dharan is a small station intended to assist British Gurkhas' operations in eastern Nepal. It is used primarily as a movement base and regional recruiting centre.

Our rooms were on the camp and my stay was surprisingly uneventful. Between work I had the best haircut ever in my life. The procedure was inclusive of a face massage, and I felt so refreshed having had the hot towel removed. We spent several weeks installing the equipment. Much of the technical stuff was done by the techs so I just provided the grunt stuff, making holes in the concrete floor in the comms centre for the radio equipment to be secured to the floor by bolts.

For the first time I saw an Atlas Moth. Beautiful, as was the scenery. On a day off we went to look at a famous temple on the banks of the Bagmati river. In my research (LOL) I see Pashupatinath Temple mentioned but no information regarding what I was told was a leper colony next door. I do remember the gold covered temple roof. I was also told westerners were not allowed in the temple.

As we looked at the crowds on the other side of the river, we encountered another monkey that took a dislike to us. Also, a Hare Krishna person sitting cross-legged on a large boulder. Eyes closed, maybe under the influence of whatever. However, made no visible reaction to us being there.

In the evenings I spent my time observing an officer who I knew from somewhere in my illustrious career. This officer was obviously involved with another man's wife and I had met a beautiful woman called Sally. I noticed Sally as she was playing tennis and we struck up a conversation and agreed to meet in the evening. The officer and I had a chat and his words to me were, "You are dangerous". After a few beers his attitude softened, and I assured him I had no interest in what he was up to. Sally and I had a few dances and nearly went further but her husband, currently in Hong Kong, had friends in the camp and I was aware the guy next door in my billet was eagle eyed. I was heading for trouble, although at one stage when Sally and another couple were heading towards the married quarters, I stood looking at her just yards from my room and as the couple went through the heavily bushed area she stood there. I knew she just needed for me to say come on but at that moment and because of my silence when the other couple shouted "Come on, Sally" she disappeared into the undergrowth. Our job finished and I was glad to return to the UK, but the memories are still there regarding Sally. By this time, I didn't care what Jen was up to in the UK. Within three years we would be divorced.

Back in Blandford, I was summoned to the office as there was a phone call for me. What now, I thought. Sgt Brown, the caller said. Yes, sir! You have been promoted to SSgt and posted to run a TA centre in Birmingham. I stood transfixed. Your posting order will be with you shortly.

What was in store for me now? The IRA was very active in Sparkbrook where the centre I was to command was based. I bid farewell to Jen and the kids and headed towards Birmingham. On arrival I met some other people I knew from previous postings. As the junior Ssgt I had various tricks inflicted on me, but things calmed down after a few weeks. The man I was replacing was selling his car, an Austin Maxi, and as I had no civilian transport, I bought it. I soon found cheap accommodation in Sparkbrook and became associated with the Territorial Soldiers. All I had to do was look after the training hall. I was introduced to Sandra my secretary and later, like so many of my women friend acquaintances, found she was in a loveless marriage (from her point of view) and her husband was always away with his work. Sat in the Sergeants' mess on exercise the local TA members were in full merriment and Sandra stood up to go to bed. A couple of the men said to me, Sandra's ready for bed! I stood there as she was just looking at me. Go on, Keith, she's ready. I was totally shocked and declined the offer and Sandra went her own way. In the office after the exercise, we never spoke about the incident, and I heard a few years later she had divorced and married another of the TA members.

I was playing badminton with a TA member in our drill hall, and he was accompanied by a woman. This woman seemed to be interested in me as I proceeded to destroy her friend and who I initially thought was her partner. Leslie Buggins, what a wonderful name. It wasn't long before we hooked up and spent a lot of time together. Both Leslie and her mother knew I was married but that did not seem to matter, and it never came up in any discussion. One weekend afternoon Leslie and I were in bed and there was a knock on my flat door. I panicked and just like in the films suggested she got under the bed. She declined. I bit the bullet as the door knocking persisted. Opening the door slightly, I found it was my landlord, who wanted to show the layout of the flat to a potential tenant. The flat above was currently under renovation, so this visit was to show him what it would look like after the work had been completed. My landlord, a woman, brushed past me as Leslie pulled up a sheet under her chin and smiled.

Oh! Said my landlord. Well, here it is, but without the woman. After a quick glance my landlord and her potential tenant left. Within a few days Leslie and her mother invited me to stay with them. I took them both on trips and to mess functions and yet never was the future discussed. Leslie's mum had a beautiful three-bedroom house, and she even brought us up a cup of tea in the mornings.

Time passed by without much trauma other than an issue regarding weapons not being returned to the armoury after an exercise. This was unknown to me as the members on returning to the TA centre were hitting the bar. I was not involved in any of their exercises. I received an irate phone call from HQ as to why they were waiting for the weapons to be returned to the armoury. The TA boys had secured the weapons somewhere and after my angry inquiry set off to return the weapons, but of course I somehow was expected to know the procedures.

Once again out of the blue came a magic phone call so I could get out of this hell hole. Staff Sergeant Brown? Yes, sir. Will you accept a posting to Saint Helena? I was overjoyed but soon to be deflated. I thought it was unusual being asked if I would accept such a posting. Thinking it was a no brainer records proceeded to push through the posting and had selected a replacement for my present post.

The job was to be a complete communications pole network and the reason I was asked rather than told regarding the posting was because my wife had to accompany me. Apparently, my wife was to be involved with the Governor's wife in various social events. Another inducement was an award of the BEM on completion of the tour. Jen currently on her nursing course refused. End of story. She was in single mode and there was no going back. I recommended one of my old corporals from my Cyprus days for the job, which I am told he accepted. Records had already told my TA replacement, so they had to put me somewhere. I requested Catterick Trade Training School. The SSgt was getting close to posting so they agreed, and so, back to Catterick. Jen and I had the house in Darlington, so it was a close commute to work, around ten miles. Norman Callender was still Group Supervisor, but Mac had been replaced by a civilian ex-serviceman called Fred Dennis. I don't know if Mac had passed or retired. I missed Mac. During my posting I had decided to get a brain back. I went to Teesside Polytechnic and gained my ONC in Electrical & Electronic Engineering. Jen by this time had joined the Army Reserve and was initially given the rank of

Lieutenant, of course unknown at that time to me. I went on to complete my HNC in the same discipline just as the Falklands war was starting. One of my Sgt instructors was called Stuart Herrington, a big man who also lived in Darlington. Following a full-dress function, I drove him back home and he suggested we drop in at his local social club for a pint.

We entered Cockerton Social Club which was full of local men enjoying a pint. As soon as they saw our uniforms they cheered, and we were bought drinks until I said I had better get home. As we left the club a great cheer went up and the chanting of "Go get them, boys" rang out. Stu, they think we are going to the Falklands. I drove him home and headed back to my life on the estate called Ridgeway.

Whist at 8 Signal Training Regt I pondered on my future and watched as member after member passed. The closest of course was Norman and I was a coffin bearer when his time came. Pete, another civilian instructor who I remember from our basic training trade course, lived in and maybe still does in Richmond, North Yorkshire. After the funeral we paid homage to Norman recalling personal actions he had taken to help us all. In one of the pubs in Richmond we sat truly sad. He had been like a father to us all. A much-liked man and a real gentleman. I try to think of the lighter side of life during these times and whatever I think may be worth mentioning. One such occasion was when a civilian instructor passed, and we were invited to the funeral. Near to the end as the vicar finished his description of the deceased's life, we all stood up to file out of the church and the speakers on full volume blasted out, "Rock Around the Clock". Apparently, the deceased loved Elvis. I apologised as I burst into laughter.

Time at home was almost at breaking point as my discharge from the army had arrived: 22 years and 100+ days. I could not believe reading my Red Book which contained my service history. I loved opening the book. The first thing that amazed me was under "Assessment of Military Conduct and Character". EXEMPLARY, and apparently my complexion was described as "FRESH". Could you imagine showing that on my CV when applying for job?!

So, back into civvy street. It never ever occurred to me to approach the Post Office or an electrical company for future work. It was my intention to join the Civil Service as a civilian instructor, but fate would intervene once more.

The Maxi car I had bought when at the TA centre in Sparkbrook gave up the ghost. There was an advert on the TV saying, "We buy any car in any condition for £400 toward the purchase of a Lada". Getting help from a scrap merchant, I purchased a maxi engine (not the gearbox) and got it home to our house in Darlington. Not having an "A" frame, the only option was drain the sump of oil, to take off the transmission and gearbox after jacking the car up. So now just the engine to get out and put the scrapyard one in. For some reason each time I tightened the bolts on the head they kept snapping. I had a torque wrench but even using the manual the bolts snapped. At three in the morning, having ignored much of the tech advice from the manual, I managed to get the car running.

Jen and I set off at a slow pace to the garage hopefully to return in our new Lada 1600cc. As we got closer to the garage, we were down to about 25 miles an hour due to the noises coming from the engine. I saw the garage just 100 yards away and then the car cut out. We coasted into the garage forecourt, finishing the last ten yards with us both pushing the lump of metal. The car dealer was all over us and we signed a new purchase of a lovely orange Lada top of the range at that time. The car dealer took my keys as I told him my old car was outside. Jen and I jumped into the Lada and positively raced out of the garage back to Darlington. The only hardship was that the steering was very heavy.

I called the Training Regiment at Catterick, enquiring about my application to be employed as an instructor. The Senior instructor at that time was called Mr Halsey. Unfortunately, there was a government moratorium going on and no new posts were currently being considered. However, I was told I would be first in line when the government was recruiting again.

Jen was furious. For six weeks I went on the dole. Reporting to the Labour exchange with proof of attempted employment. Checking with Mr Halsey I was told it could be six months or more.

I had to get an income as we had the mortgage and all the other bills to pay, and Jennifer only offered once to pay a month's rates.

I searched in the papers and there it was. I went to London for an interview. In the lift another man struck up a conversation with me and enquired what floor I was going to. I told him and he said, ok good luck and curiously "see you later".

I entered the office, and a very efficient woman greeted me and asked who I had the appointment with. I was aware that sometimes it is the way an applicant conducts himself before an interview and may well rest on the secretary's impression. As a sort of pre-interview that may make the difference as to whether you got the job or not. She was very attractive, but I kept myself in check and sat on a chair waiting to be summoned. Mr Brown? I looked up and it was the man I had met in the lift. He introduced himself as Major ******. We went through my qualifications. He looked at my Red Book. The contract was outlined along with pay and length of contract etc.

I signed the contract and was now a Warrant Officer in the Sultan of Oman's Army. I waited for the date to fly out. Jen said, It's for two years. Yes, I said, but I phoned Mr Halsey, and he said the moratorium may go on for quite a few months. Anyway, I could resign from my new contract anytime I wanted. The only thing was I may lose part of my lump sum at the end of my contract. I was now in the Sultan of Oman's Army.

I boarded the train on my way to the airport and that was the first time I ever saw a tear in Jen's eye.

On arrival in Oman everyone was in line and excited. I chatted to a guy called Terry who had never been in the armed forces at all, yet here he was as a technician Sergeant in the Sultan of Oman's 1st Signal Regiment.

I was looking forward to meeting Danny Flanigan, a well-known ex-Royal Signals man. "You don't know how glad I am to see you," he said. I was introduced to another Warrant Officer Class 1 and another Warrant officer 2. Neither had served in another army but had GPO qualifications. Day one in "SEEB" camp about seven miles from Muscat. I got my uniform into the tailors. In the next few days Danny and I travelled around the regiment and accommodation area to familiarize me as to our realm.

As usual I was in second rate accommodation a portacabin about half a mile from Danny's flat in the main compound. I was introduced to my Oman Sergeant who spoke very good English as he had in a previous life lived for three years in Middlesbrough. Unbelievable, as I sit here punching these keys here in Normanby, Middlesbrough.

One perk of the job was to be able to take on private jobs for cash. Danny took me to Al Azaiba Camp which is the depot of the Sultan's Special Forces. Danny introduced me to Captain Jim Farmer who was to become a buddy of mine and a bit mad. More later. Danny and I did a couple of underground cable jobs in the camp and was amply compensated.

I read the book written by an SAS colonel about the Dhofar War also known as the Omani Civil War.

Lots of countries involved and a book worth reading. Basically, the old Sultan was ousted by his son "Qaboos bin Said" and his mother, assisted by the British. The old sultan had the backing of the Russians and the Chinese and some South Yemen. Naturally the SAS were involved. Finally, the Shah of Iran intervened and supported Qaboos and the war ended.

A quick story also in the book but I met the man involved. Danny and I had just finished another cable job for Jim, and he took us into the Communications Centre. Sat there was a Captain in a wheelchair. I mention him because the story goes that the SAS had been caught in an ambush during that war. I believe at that time the man was a L/Cpl anyway. He had been shot in the back, so his mates put him onto the wing of their Land Rover as there was no room elsewhere. They were trying to get out of this firefight. Some people know when they are dying and say things like "I'm going". That is exactly what the shot man started to say. "NO! hang on ,mate, we are nearly out of this." Just as they were getting clear the injured L/Cpl repeated saying 'I am going". Not far now, mate, soon get you to the hospital. NO! I'm going to fall off this F—king wing! That man was now a Captain and was given lifetime employment by the Sultan.

To stay out of trouble, I used to visit Danny in the main block, and we binge-watched "Shogun" with Richard Chamberlain. We did have the odd hot-tub evening in which the nurses employed in the hospital also enjoyed, but for once I never saw any sexual play. As I press keys to the keyboard, I realise how old I am with such a description. I was to get more familiar with the hospital staff very soon.

I visited one of the exchanges and was introduced to the civilian staff who were also contractors but as they seemed to think above us military. As we chatted, I became very thirsty and went into the back room where there was a sink. It was filthy and looked like it had never been used. Stupidly I turned the tap and water flowed. I cupped my hands and quenched my thirst.

A day or two later I had a small cable to joint in a cable pit. I opened the pit cover and hundreds of cockroaches scampered around the wet interior. The job was small, and I finished in less than an hour, but I noticed a cable that had fallen off one of the cable bearers and in the sitting position I leaned forward and tried to lift the lead covered cable back onto the bearer. The cable was about half an inch from the curved lip of the cable bearer but was resisting. I was not going to stand up knee deep in water and cockroaches. I made even more effort to get the cable into place. Now considering my years of back injuries I should have had more sense. My bloody mindedness prevailed and just when the cable found its rightful resting place, I felt this intense pain in the lower part of my stomach. I literately crawled to my Toyota van, having closed the cable pit cover and pulled myself onto the seat. The pain was intense as I put my foot on the clutch to get the van into gear. On the move towards the hospital that was quite close I left the van in second gear and eventually parked up outside the Emergency entrance. Danny was informed by phone, but I was left on a trolley in the corridor. I was dozing off as the pain had subsided only to be awoken by a nurse putting a thermometer in my mouth. The nurse disappeared and I was being trolleyed to a medical ward.

The nurse who was in charge in the medical ward put me onto a drip and blood was taken. Apparently, I had Shigella Dysentery. That sink, I think. My own fault, yet nobody seemed to address my stomach issue. After my treatment was complete and my complaining about my stomach was listened to, I was transferred to the surgical ward.

The consultant and one of his surgeons felt around and quickly concluded I had a hernia. So, a day later I was lying in bed opposite an old Omani man who looked to be in his late seventies. Of course, he had two hernias according to him. The nurses came in and wheeled him away. I gave him the thumbs up. On return he was back opposite me and smiling. On coming to, like most of us do, I looked under the sheets to see if anything had been done.

Next minute my Arab friend was out of bed and off to the toilet. I dozed off and when I awoke found he was gone.

There were no nurses at the nurse station but as the old man had undergone surgery for two hernias I couldn't be outdone and walked quite slowly to the toilet. Eventually when a nurse appeared, and I said I had managed to get to the toilet she went crazy. "WHAT!" she screamed at me. I replied that the old man had managed, and he had two hernias. She informed me that the old man had NOT had his surgery, and I was to stay in bed for several days.

As the consultant looked at my bright red stomach, he cut some stitches and proceeded to inject into my stomach a foamy substance, possibly cortisone, that erupted from my stomach like a volcanic eruption. Again, my luck was not as good as I would have liked. I had caught an infection from a dirty surgical implement. Interestingly, the wound was never restitched as we waited for the body to heal itself. However, near to discharge there was a material soaked in a bleach liquid that I saw a nurse mix from powder form. Having had the padding secured with Elastoplast, I was discharged. As I walked down the corridor to some transport awaiting outside to take me back to my accommodation, my stomach started to burn like crazy. I went into the nearest toilet. Inside the booth I dropped my trousers to find my bright blue underpants were almost entirely white. I ripped off the padding and off I went. The pain subsided and eventually, with stomach closed, I awaited my next torment. Just as I was exiting the hospital, I bumped into my Arab teacher, a Captain who I had met on my basic Arab course. He had a real sense of humour. He told me he was in hospital due to the "Little Green Can" habit. He was talking about Heineken, which apparently had led him into alcohol dependability. I wished him good luck and said, "We should meet up again for a drink once you have recovered".

Jim and I went to the airport bar and watched the Air Jockeys (pilots on the overnight layover) chat up the air hostesses. Never mind they were flying out the next day and carrying many lives in their hands. I whispered into Jim's ear, telling him what I thought of these irresponsible airline pilots although that is not my exact wording to Jim. As we watched, Jim was getting a little agitated especially as the women were of course very attractive. We were not included in their company and Jim suggested we went back to camp and get a couple of weapons, return, and waste these arseholes. Now I don't know if it was a test to see my reaction as we had discussed my possible application to join his unit. Now I had made no such application, but Jim seemed to think I would be a good fit for the unit. I took Jim back to his unit and decided to keep him at a distance for a while. Later, when chatting to Jim, he told me he had a place in Costa Rica, and he was married. When I left Oman eventually, I was told he was in jail in South Africa. So somehow, he had become even more a mercenary than previously.

One Sgt who was a technician and never been in the military but had become a friend, Terry, came with me to pick up my Major Omani boss for a private job on his farm. The idea was to lay some small diameter cable ducting above the surface with holes drilled with the ducting attached to a pump to water whatever he was trying to grow. I had Boney M in the cassette just below the dashboard. The device was not playing but was switched on; of course as soon as we started so did the recording. The major was startled as the volume was at full blast. Oh, is that satellite? said the OC. Terry and I burst out laughing. We just could not look at the man. I switched the radio off and realised how much real-world education these people needed. It didn't matter if you had so much money to buy the expert knowledge and procurement of equipment, they needed modern world education because one day the oil will run out.

Part of the contract made allowance for a week of return to the UK or have your loved ones sent out. Jen arrived and we entered the reserved hut for us holidaymakers. Basically, there was just a bedroom and a shower/toilet. We were off that first night to Seeb and a restaurant that I had eaten at before. No serviettes so an old heavy sink much like the one I caught dysentery in, to wash your hands, as of course there was no cutlery. Fingers only. Surprisingly, Jen dived in, and she really did enjoy the meal. We returned to our accommodation and Jen jumped in the shower and switched the contraption on. Water cascaded from the showerhead and immediately half the population of Oman's cockroaches swarmed out of the drainage pipe. I shouted and as usual Jen took no notice and looking down casually stepped out of the shower. I then proceeded to get rid of them in every which way I could. Later that night we could hear the cockroaches in the walls and possibly in the ceiling. Lying there in the dark, hearing the scratching, I jumped out of bed as something fell on my face. Having put the light on I found it was just a flake of paint from the ceiling. Much of the week was spent introducing Jen to everyone and sightseeing. The week was coming to an end. I had just one more year left before I had to decide what to do as I had not received any news from the UK about the moratorium. Jen flew back home and unknown to me was running up quite a debt.

I was detached to a fort which contained the Minister for Defence who was a brother of the Sultan. In the courtyard was a brand-new Aston Martin DB6. I could smell the leather even with the doors closed. The chauffeur was walking around this beautiful car with a duster. We had a quick chat and I got to work with a wiring job.

The car encounter reminded me of the Sultan's horse training manager. A very well-known horse trainer in the UK, who had stables there. He was quite famous, and he had successfully won many events. The racing season was underway, so he asked the Sultan to be granted UK leave to manage his horses at home for a few weeks. However, the Middle East horse racing season was also about to open, and the Sultan was keen to win as many races as possible (not him personally as the races were for horses only). One Sunday afternoon someone from the palace arrived at the stables. The trainer was asked to reconsider his request and would he accompany the envoy to a BMW garage. The trainer said, "But it is Sunday, the garage won't be open." The envoy turned and smiled and said, "Oh yes it will". In a short amount of time the trainer was driving his brand-new top range BMW back to the stables. The trainer stayed. I am not privy to how many races the Sultan's horses won but experience light bribery myself.

I had been in the 1st Signal Regt just over 20 months. "Excitement". Caught in a flash flood when transporting a GPO high up visitor through the UAE en route to the Sultan's Tank Regiment. Water very close to the door handles of my Toyota van and successfully traversing what should have been a dry wadi was now worthy of being an international Canoeing Slalom Course. I could see the panic in his eyes as I entered the river. I smiled – after all, for me it was an adventure. My adventure seen by maybe 30 people on the other side of the river was going to plan and I knew the river was now only three feet at its deepest and should we not be able to drive up the slight incline to the other side of the bank many hands would be able to push us onto the bank.

On return to my home regiment, I enquired about work with the GPO and our visitor said he would employ me and with thanks he left, and I wondered how I would maybe be asking for an extension should my elusive UK civil service call never come through during my current contract.

The rain was pouring down and Terry and I were playing golf. There was no grass, so we were driving to BROWNS instead of GREENS. As we neared the end, we came across two nurses. They were on their way back to their accommodation. Long story short I ended up on a more than friendly basis with one of them. I won't mention her name because what happened was tragic, but she was Scottish. I will refer to her as the "wee lassie". Maybe I have remembered the events out of sequence, but I was not in Oman (luckily for me) when the tragic event took place. Our relationship was short and neither of us felt regret upon parting as I was too focused on getting back to the UK.

After us parting she latched onto a civilian contractor who lived in a portacabin. She truly fell in love; however, not so the contractor. Now the wee lassie never smoked. That is important as later, it was a suggestion from the defence that she had fallen asleep, and a cigarette caused the fire. The story goes she had fallen asleep in the portacabin when her new boyfriend went to the civilian club. It was later confirmed she was locked in. Word went around that she had threatened to tell the man's wife about their affair, and she was to marry him after his divorce. Two detectives from Scotland questioned the man and apparently, they could not get a confession. I still question WHY she was locked in. With no formal UK involvement, he did go to jail but under the Omani law of having committed adultery. He was sentenced to one year in jail.

The most challenging time in Oman was Ramadan. From dawn to dusk no water or food should pass the lips of the population. During the day my men were tired because when dusk arrived, they were up all night feeding their faces and drinking and getting little sleep, and the cycle continued for 30 days. I had a big cable to be pulled in by hand, and complaint after complaint of how tired they were was to some extent quelled by my Sergeant, but I had reached my limit. I said I was trying to help their country and if they didn't care then nor did I.

I stomped into the office and Danny said, "What's up?" I said I had had it up to my ears and I was resigning my post. We walked into the OC's office, and I explained I wanted to resign from my contract. The OC was trying to do his best to stop me leaving by offering me Warrant Officer One promotion and to oversee the construction unit in Salalah. I don't think Keith is going to accept, said Danny. No, I didn't. Awaiting to see if I had lost my lump sum payout at the end of my contract, I was sceptical, but I did get 21/24ths of my contracted bonus.

Waiting for my flight, a phone call came for me and it was Catterick. Could I come into 8 Signal Regt Training School for an interview? At last, some good news. I was so excited.

Now back in the UK I found Jen had sold the Lada because the steering was so heavy and bought a new Toyota Corolla and somehow got it in my name. Also, we were £2,000 in debt at the bank. All this after I was sending home almost that each month. The end was coming.

I entered the room following my interview with Mr Halsey. His only words were "Just pass the exam". I did.

Initially I was sent to Line Group to teach Basic Electrical Principles. Later and after some Senior Instructors' interview clashes, I secured my place as a tech instructor and rose to the dizzy heights teaching advance principles.

Jen was hitting the nightclubs with no pretence as to having a night out with the girls. Cars would pull up during the evening and Jen would be all dolled up. Racing out the door and the cars screeching down the road in case I assume they thought I would see who was with her.

All was about to get nasty. The kids were sat in the front room and as Jen came down the stairs, I threw a load of pamphlets onto the table about coping with divorce and such advice.

The phone was ringing, and her lawyer was apparently on the attack. I offered £185 per month and offered to pay the mortgage as I had done for years, along with most of the utilities, but she had never paid towards any house purchase or upkeep ever in all those years except one rates payment after I said we are struggling!

We sold the house and split the proceeds. I bought a beautiful house in Catterick Village, at that time for £22,000 with a 100% mortgage. She bought a terraced house in Darlington. With the divorce acrimony still in full motion, Jen had managed to have an issue with our eldest daughter, Karen.

Karen came to live with me for a short time. Again, following the divorce, Jen took me back to court for more support. Her solicitor questioned how I could afford a £22,000 house and she needed more money to support her and the children. Now, the judge sat alongside us and said he did not believe that a house cost of £22,000 in "this day and age" was unreasonable. The judge awarded Jen £5.00 for costs of looking after the children and I was awarded £5.00 also. I mentioned to the judge that I did make an offer initially to my wife, but she said her solicitor had said she deserved more and as soon as I heard that I withdrew the offer. I then said to myself "I have had enough". The judge was just getting ready to finish when I said, "Excuse me, your honour. My wife has been claiming children's allowance for my daughter Karen who lives with me." Is that true, Mrs Brown? She admitted that it was true. I went on to say, that dates to last May and I cannot claim that in retrospect. I had done my homework. Is that true, Mrs Brown? Yes, she said. You will hand the allowance book for Karen back to Mr Brown.

So, she came in all guns blazing with her solicitor looking for more free cash and left having to pay me. Result! A month or two later Karen went back because she was bringing home men and partying, and I was not getting too much sleep, so I put my foot down and she went back to Jen.

When you have had an eventful life such as mine (not that I have done a survey), I thought nothing more would be so eventful as my past life. How wrong I was. After 19 years in the Civil Service, I had several liaisons, trying to find a partner that I wouldn't wish on anyone. The events that followed. Another girlfriend that liked to party.

Three more wives. An alcoholic, a vegan from hell and a Bi-polar woman initially in a wheelchair with a three-legged dog called Dawson. Fourteen years living in America in the beautiful state of Maine.

I wonder if I have had a full life, but if not, my new dog Ruby, a rescue from Northern Ireland, is loyal and my old Army buddy and his wife are still visiting me and will be taking me out on Sunday for my 79th birthday. Thank you, John and Joan, for looking after Ruby as I now tour the world…because I can.

The End or is it?